D1570829

THE TRUTH HURTS
BY JIMMY PIERSALL

WITH RICHARD WHITTINGHAM

CONTEMPORARY
BOOKS, INC.
CHICAGO

Library of Congress Cataloging in Publication Data

Piersall, Jimmy
    The truth hurts.

    Includes Index
    1. Piersall, Jimmy.   2. Baseball players—United
States—Biography.   I. Whittingham, Richard, 1939–
II. Title.
GV865.P54A37   1985   796.357'092'4 [B]   84-23103
ISBN 0-8092-5377-1

Published by Contemporary Books, Inc.
180 North Michigan Avenue, Chicago, Illinois 60601
Manufactured in the United States of America
Library of Congress Catalog Card Number: 84-23103
International Standard Book Number: 0-8092-5377-1

Published simultaneously in Canada by Beaverbooks, Ltd.
195 Allstate Parkway, Valleywood Business Park
Markham, Ontario L3R 4T8 Canada

CONTENTS

To my friends over the years
who understand me and
take me for what I am

THE TRUTH HURTS

"Trouble follows me."
                    Billy Martin, 1977

"Me, too."
                    Jimmy Piersall, 1983

They were throwing batteries, golf balls. I mean they were really going at it. The umpire stopped the game, and it took them 20 minutes to clean up the field. Bill McKinley was the umpire at second base, and he came out to me in center field and said. "You're an instigator, Piersall." "I don't know what you're talking about, McKinley," I said. "All I do know is that they shot the wrong McKinley." And he threw me out of the game.

1
COMING BACK

Probably the best thing that ever happened to me was going nuts. It brought people out to the ballpark to get a look at me, and they came to the places where I was invited to speak. "Let's see what the monkey looks like," they'd say, and they'd come by the thousands. And in all the businesses I got involved with it helped because the people I was promoting things to or selling products to knew about me because of all the publicity about my mental problems. That was back in the early 1950s. It's pretty much the same today, in the 1980s; they still want to see what the monkey is like.

To this day, the first thing people ask my wife Jan, or other people who know me, is, "Is he really goofy?" or "What's he really like?"—meaning "Is he really crazy?" They've been doing that for more than 30 years now. It doesn't bother me. The way I look at it, it's been a blessing for me. I am a nonconformist, an individualist. I tell it like I see it, even though it's gotten me into a helluva lot of

THE TRUTH HURTS

trouble with everybody from Charlie Finley to Eddie Einhorn and Jerry Reinsdorf. I am not a blind follower of rules and regulations. I tell the truth, even if it hurts, which you'll see as you read this book.

Nineteen fifty-three was the year I came back to baseball. A lot of people didn't think I'd make it back, not after all that had gone on the year before, the things I did on the field, the stay in the mental hospital—all that. The sportswriters especially. The attitude of most of them was one big doubt after another: Let's see what he can do. Let's see what mistake he's going to make. Let's see if he's going to get mad. Let's see if he's going to blow up. Let's see if he can take the pressure of it all. There was one exception, however. That was Roger Birtwell of the *Boston Globe*, who was very supportive; his attitude about my making a successful comeback was very positive. He was the only one who stayed by me.

To be honest, I didn't know whether I could handle it. There were a lot of pressures I knew I would have to endure. And I knew one little slip and it would be all over. I realized all that. I also had a lot of fears: whether I could catch a ball again, whether I could throw it like I used to, whether I could even hit it. At the same time I knew that if I performed, got the job done on the field, I'd be back for good. But I was very worried.

At the time I was also afraid to face people. I didn't know how they would react to me or what they would say to me. I talked to Tom Yawkey, the Red Sox owner, about it, and he seemed to understand what I was going through. He said he knew it was a difficult time for me. But he made it clear that he had faith that I could make it back. So he made a decision to send me down to Florida early, a couple of months before spring training. The Red Sox paid for me and my whole family to go down there so I could work out.

4

I had all those different fears at that time in my life, had had them ever since I'd gotten out of the hospital. I went down there to work them out.

One of our coaches, George Susce, lived down there in Sarasota where we had our spring training camp. Mr. Yawkey wanted me to work with him. George was a good coach and a terrific guy. All the players loved him. They called him "Good Kid" because that's what he called everybody else. He didn't pay attention to anybody's name, just called everyone "Good Kid." It was like Ted Williams calling a lot of people "Bush" because he couldn't remember their first names.

I told him about the fears I had: whether I could catch the ball, throw it, hit it. He told me not to worry about it. "You work, and you'll be in right field on opening day," he told me. Throughout those days he built a lot of confidence in me with his attitude. He was tough, a real hard worker himself, and that's what he expected of the ball players. We went out to Payne Field, and he'd hit me fly balls day after day. I ran, batted, and got myself in damn good shape. Payne Field, coincidentally, is the same place the White Sox use today for spring training.

Another thing that helped a lot was taking up the game of golf. I'd never swung a golf club until I got down to Sarasota. But I had some time when I wasn't working out with Susce, and I'd also gotten a set of clubs the year before. I got them from Hillerich & Bradsby, the company that makes baseball bats. I'd endorsed something for them, and in those days they paid you that way. They'd put your name on a bat and give you a set of golf clubs. No big dollars like they do today. So I went out and tried the game and found I liked it. I played a lot and discovered that it helped me get rid of my fear of meeting people. I played on the public course there with all kinds of different people. Some of them were retired and living down there, others

5

were just townspeople. They didn't know who I was, and they didn't care about it. They were all friendly, and I was at ease with them.

Between George Susce and playing golf, my life got turned around that year.

When the other players came down for spring training, they were very good to me too. They treated me just like anybody else, which is exactly what I wanted.

Ted Williams also came back that year—1953—from his hitch in Korea. He didn't join the club until later in the season, but the thought of his coming back and my playing in the same outfield with him was just tremendous. He'd been my idol for maybe 12 or 13 years by then, from the time I was a little kid.

Back when I was about 10 or 11, I sold newspapers in Waterbury, Connecticut, where we lived. If you sold the most papers or got a certain number of new customers, you'd get a free ticket to go see the Yankees play on Sunday. Well, I used to win that a lot, especially when I knew the Red Sox and Ted Williams were coming to town. I worked like hell for it because they were my heroes.

I'd earn the ticket, and then I'd go down to Yankee Stadium early so I could watch batting practice. I used to have a little camera of my mother's and I'd take it along. I'd get as close as I could to watch Ted Williams take batting practice, and I'd take pictures of him.

When the game started I'd sit out in the right field seats. One day I was sitting behind a little elderly lady. She had a big hat on, I remember. Anyway, Ted hit a home run that day. It landed in the seats right near where we were. The ball bounced up and knocked her hat off. Everybody went for the ball, especially me, but the lady got it. I said, "Lady, please give me the ball." I mean it was *Ted Williams's home run ball.* "Lady, I'll come up and clean your house. Anything!" But she wouldn't give me the ball.

Then, to think, 10 years later I was playing in the big

leagues with Ted Williams, on the same team, in the same outfield. I was 21, and he was 33 or 34. It was incredible, something I'd dreamed about as a kid, and it had actually come true.

I'd come up at the end of the 1950 season. Williams didn't have a lot of time for me then. He'd broken his elbow in the All-Star game that year and wasn't playing. But when I did talk to him or ask him something he was always very nice to me.

In spring training in 1952, when I came back up with the Red Sox, I started to face some of the great curveball pitchers, like Vic Raschi and Allie Reynolds and Eddie Lopat of the Yankees and Feller, Garcia, and Wynn of the Indians, and I was having a lot of trouble hitting them. I remember Ted came up to me in the batting cage one day and said, "If you don't learn to hit the breaking stuff, kid, and learn to keep your head in there, you might as well grab yourself a pail and go to work somewhere else because you'll never keep a job here. You've *got* to keep your head in there." I knew what he meant, but sticking your head in there with pitchers like Bob Feller, well, it wasn't all that easy. Anyway, Ted went off to the Korean War just after that and didn't play for us in 1952. I never forgot the advice, though, and one day I went to Johnny Pesky and said, "John, how in hell am I going to keep my head in there?"

"Easy," he said. "Just put your chin on your left shoulder and lean in."

I did it, and it worked; in fact, I got to the point where I never took my chin off my shoulder. Later I read in Ted's book that he mentioned that I was the one guy whom he really worried about getting hit in the head because I kept my head in there all the time. He didn't mention that he was the one who told me to do it.

Ted used to give a lot of good advice about hitting. He used to say, "Quick with your hands, hands and wrists,

7

keep your eye on the ball, learn the strike zone, hit strikes, don't try to overpower the ball. When you're in a slump, think about up the middle, right center, left center. Learn to wait on the ball. Learn what pitchers throw, what their best pitches are. Don't walk up there with nothing on your mind; know what you're going to be swinging at." I used to keep notebooks on pitchers I'd be facing. I always followed Ted's advice. I know that really helped me. I think I ended up with 18 notebooks filled about pitchers. Williams made me realize one important thing: if I was going to survive in the big leagues, especially after I hurt my arm and couldn't throw like I used to, I had to become a better hitter. I had to become a tough out.

When Williams came back from Korea in 1953, after I'd had my troubles, he treated me just as if nothing had happened. When you've had a mental problem or been an alcoholic, when you're over it, you just want to be treated like anybody else, and that's what he did. Oh, he'd needle me, give me a hard time—not about my problem but about ordinary things. He liked to have fun. But he treated me normally, and this was very important to me when I was coming back.

When Ted got back, he wasn't put into the lineup right away, but people came out to the ballpark just to see him pinch-hit and take batting practice. We'd draw 30,000 in Boston on a weekday just to see him take a couple of swings. In fact, his first time up he pinch-hit a home run off Mike Garcia. Then, when he got back into the lineup, everywhere we went he packed them in.

I remember one game in particular against the Tigers. Ted was in left field, and I was in center. About 50,000 people in Detroit turned out. The game was in the ninth inning, and the score was tied. Harvey Kuenn was the hitter, and Fred Hatfield was on second base. Now, I was playing shallow for Harvey; I used to play shallow a lot anyway. Harvey used to hit to right center field, and I often used to move as the ball was being pitched. I liked to move so he wasn't sure what I was going to do. Well, sure in hell, he hit a line drive to right center, and fortunately I'd gotten a jump on it because I'd been moving to my left on the pitch. I caught it and doubled Hatfield off second.

Then we went to the top of the 10th, and we had the bases loaded. I came up at the plate, and the count went to three balls, no strikes. I looked off to the side at Del Baker, our third base coach, and he gave me the sign to take, take the pitch. I did. It was a strike. With the count three and one, Del signaled to take it again. You could take it a lot in those days. They had a different theory on the situation then, especially if you were the lead-off hitter. Today the lead-off hitters strike out a hundred times in a season. That's ridiculous. Anyway, the next pitch was not too close, but John Flaherty, the umpire, called it a strike.

I stepped out of the box and took a look at him. I didn't like the call. The next pitch I couldn't have hit with a five iron, but he called me out! Well, I turned around and gave him holy hell. I gave him a thousand words in a minute. He wouldn't throw me out of the game because he knew he had blown it. But what could I do about it?

I went out to the outfield for the bottom of the 10th. The fans were hollering and swearing, and I just smiled up at them. Didn't do a thing; I didn't give them the finger, nothing; I just smiled. Then, all of a sudden, they were throwing wine bottles, those dark brown bottles that all the winos drink. And they threw paper cups with ice in them. They shot paper clips and hit me behind the shoulder. One guy threw a hammer that had "Fuck you" written on it. They were throwing batteries, golf balls. I mean they were really going at it.

The umpire stopped the game, and it took them 20 minutes to clean up the field. Bill McKinley was the umpire at second base, and he came out to me in center field and said, "You're an instigator, Piersall."

9

THE TRUTH HURTS

"I don't know what you're talking about, McKinley," I said. "All I do know is that they shot the wrong McKinley." And he threw me out of the game.

The next day in the paper, Rick Farrell, the Tigers' general manager, said I brought all of that stuff out on the field myself and dropped it. Can you imagine that? He said *I* brought the stuff out on the field and dropped it. Of all the general managers I've known, Farrell has to be credited with the all-time most stupid statement I've ever heard—that I brought the hammer out, that I brought the batteries out.

From then on, when I'd go to Detroit they had cartoons in the paper about me in center field throwing stuff around. The hostility was so bad, though, that they had to put security guards up in the center field bleachers.

It was Ted Williams who brought the fans out, good ones and bad ones. They came to see him play. Just as I had idolized Ted as a kid, I admired him when I got to know him as a person. He was so hardworking, such an individualist, a perfectionist. He couldn't stand failure. He was tight-lipped a lot of the time and a loner, but he found ways of getting things out of his system. He'd never get an ulcer; instead, he'd give one. He told me never to hold it in, never to let it get at me. I learned from him. That's why I've always popped my beak to get it out, so that it didn't stay inside of me.

Ted was unpredictable, though. There was one situation I'll never forget. When Ted was mad or giving somebody a hard time or just kidding around, he'd talk through his clenched teeth, very gruff. If we were all excited about something and talking about it, he'd say through his teeth, "Big deal, Bush. What a thrill, Bush." He did it all the time.

One day, however, we were in New York to play the Yankees, and he was going to be on the "Ed Sullivan Show" that night. Well, he was all excited about that, and before the game he was talking to this pretty girl in the box seats next to our dugout. He was telling her about being on Ed Sullivan's show, and I heard him, so I hollered out to him from the dugout, "Big deal, Bush. What a thrill, Bush."

Boy, he got furious with me, really furious. He stormed down into the dugout and grabbed me and lifted me up. He was going to hang me on one of those hooks in the dugout. "Hey, you better put me down," I said.

He said, "Well, don't *you* talk to me anymore. No more at all."

Well, I didn't know what to do. I'd only been trying to give it back to him like he gave it to us. But the rest of the year he didn't talk to me. Not a word. I was really hurt that I had created the problem. But I hadn't meant to.

I remember a time later that year when we were playing in Baltimore and it was tied 0–0 in the eighth. Ted was in left, and Gus Triandos hit a drive down the left field line. It hit the foul line, which was wooden and painted white in those days, and rolled along it all the way to the fence where the line made a turn. Well, the ball made the turn and followed it along the fence. Ted had to chase it down the foul line and then around in front of the fence to left-center field. Triandos, who was slow as hell, got a home run inside the park, and they won the ball game with that run.

The next day Del Baker, who was really a great coach and a well-respected man, started getting all over me for not getting the ball after it was rolling in front of the fence in left-center. Why didn't I get over from center field and get it? I said, "Hey, the ball was on the left field line, in *left* field. Why don't you start getting on him?" I pointed at Ted. He looked back at me, and there was this kind of stunned silence. You see, everyone was very careful with Ted, how they talked to him. Nobody would ordinarily say something like that to him or get on him for something. Well, he didn't even say anything to me then. Just glared, then turned away and ignored me.

11

THE TRUTH HURTS

The next spring, however, we were in Sarasota, Florida. It was the beginning of spring training, and I was sitting in the locker room, reading my mail. Ted walked up and said, "Hey, Bush, this may be the kid's last season. Let's have a good year together."

"Sure," I said.

He slapped me on the back and said. "Everything's gonna be all right, kid," and that was it. All forgotten. We got along fine, and Ted had a great year, batting .388 and leading the league. I had a pretty good year myself. Ted treated me well from that point on. He told me that he respected me as a fielder, and I, of course, respected him as a great ball player. We played together through 1958, and then I was traded to the Indians.

Nineteen fifty-three was also the year I became good friends with Billy Martin, and we've remained that way to this day. Billy was playing second base for the Yankees that year and was the big star of the World Series. He hit .500 in it, two home runs, eight RBIs; he won it for the Yankees in '53.

We had had a fight the year before that was pretty well publicized, but I don't remember a lot about it, just as I don't remember a lot about the other things that happened the year when I was sick. I draw pretty much of a blank when it comes to all the things I did in 1952. It wasn't a big deal, though; just a scuffle under the stands at Fenway Park. In those days both teams had to go through the same dugout to get to their dressing rooms. I guess after one game we exchanged some words on the way out and got into it. The only one who got hurt, however, was Bill Dickey, the old Yankee catcher who was a coach for them then. He tried to break it up and ended up with a few stitches in his foot for the effort.

When I came back in '53, Billy came up before our first game with the Yankees and asked how I was. Then he wished me well. I knew he meant it, and it meant a helluva lot to me. Billy is a very human individual, sensitive and, like me, easily offended. He doesn't want to hurt anybody, but he's a battler. He's also one of the least understood persons in the world and one of the most courageous I've ever met. He's in a fishbowl all the time. Everywhere he goes, everything he does, everybody's eyes are on him. Talk about pressure. But Billy Martin is good for baseball, and he'll always have a job because he brings people out to the ballpark. I found out what kind of class guy he is that afternoon in 1953 when we played the Yankees.

There were some other good friends on the Red Sox the year I came back, like Ted Lepcio, Dick Gernert, Clyde Vollmer, Ellis Kinder. Milt Bolling was my roommate. Milt was a very nice, easygoing kind of guy. I was high-strung, and he was low-key, but we got along just fine. Neither of us smoked or drank. He had a tough break, though—hurt his foot, and it affected his career. Milt stayed with the game and has been a scout for Boston since the 1950s.

Ellis Kinder had a great year in 1953, 27 saves. Ellis was a heavy drinker, and sometimes when he'd walk by me in right field on his way in from the bullpen his breath would almost knock me over. He'd reach over to me and say, "Be ready, kid; I'm gonna pitch those right-handers away. They're gonna start hitting 'em out this way now." And I'll be a son of a buck if he wouldn't get them to do it. When he said it, damned if the balls didn't come out to right field. He'd pitch the batters away, and they'd hit line ropes to right. He was also a great change-up pitcher. I really liked Ellis a lot. But he had a tough life. He died far too young, of hardening of the arteries, I believe it was.

Mel Parnell was there that year, too. He was a class guy from New Orleans and a great competitor. He won 21 games for us that year. He had a great sinker-slider. The index finger on his pitching hand had been broken and wasn't quite normal, so when he threw the ball it would automatically become a slider. I liked to play behind him

13

because he was always ahead of the batters. He was the opposite of somebody like Maury McDermott, who was always 3 and 0, 3 and 1, 2 and 0.

I remember the no-hitter Mel hurled against the White Sox in 1956. One reason I remember it is because I saved it for him by making a diving catch of a line drive hit by Luis Aparicio. Another is that when the final out was hit back to him by Walt Dropo, who was with Chicago then, instead of throwing it to first, Mel ran over with it himself and stepped on the bag. When you think about it, the no-hitter was quite a feat because Mel was a left-hander and Fenway Park had that short porch in left field, 315 down the line and only about 340 in left-center.

George Kell, who later made the Hall of Fame, played third base for us that year. He was always very friendly. I really respected him as a great hitter. He had come over the year before from Detroit in a trade for Johnny Pesky and a bunch of other guys. He was a big help to me. I used to ride in with him to Fenway Park in Boston because we lived out in the same area. He tried to help me understand how to react to certain things and how not to overreact. He'd impress upon me that sometimes you had to live with the bad as well as the good, that sometimes you just had to accept things. He'd say there were 154 ball games a year and you were bound to have some bad ones, but not to worry about them. Just get over them, he'd say, and go on and keep working. George became a good broadcaster after he left the game. He's been doing the Tiger games in Detroit for about 25 years.

Lou Boudreau was our manager in 1953, and he had finally come to understand that I didn't like to or want to play shortstop, the position he had tried to convert me to the year before. I'd been an all-star center fielder for four years in the minor leagues, and he tried to make me into a shortstop. That was one of the things that contributed to all my problems. I couldn't adjust to it. Some guys don't mind going from one position to another, but most can't do it. I was one of the latter. Now, in 1953, Boudreau and one of our coaches, Bill McKechnie, decided I would be best in the outfield, the position I was by far most comfortable in.

I did not like Boudreau as a manager. I could never understand why he put me at shortstop, why he piled on the pressures. Another thing I can't forgive him for occurred at spring training the following year, 1954. My wife was pregnant, and it was going to be a breech birth. I asked him if I could go home to be with her, to help if I could, but he wouldn't let me go. Then, when I first wore the batting helmet, he told me I was gutless, that I would be shy at the plate. He was a great ball player but never a good manager.

I was unsure of myself at the start of spring training in 1953. I worried a lot about making it. But then one day we played the Dodgers. They'd won the National League pennant the year before, and they'd win it again that year. They had a wonderful team: Jackie Robinson was at second, Gil Hodges at first, PeeWee Reese at short, Bobby Cox at third, Roy Campanella catching, and Duke Snider, Carl Furillo, and Gene Hermanski in the outfield. Carl Erskine was pitching for them that day, and I went five for five. I also made some good catches out in right field. From that time on I felt I could start in right field.

And I did. Dom DiMaggio was still in center field, at least in spring training. But he was 36 years old by then, and he quit the game shortly afterward. Tommy Umphlett was getting more time out there than Dom was, and the writing seemed to be on the wall. Dominic was a quiet, soft-spoken guy whom you could not help but love. Boudreau handled that situation badly, too. Here was Dom DiMaggio with a lifetime batting average of .298, who had been a standout center fielder for the Red Sox for 11 years, really a great player. And Boudreau treated him poorly and forced him to quit. I didn't like that.

THE TRUTH HURTS

The fans in Boston were terrific and made me feel very much at home. On the road, they weren't always so nice. Occasionally somebody would shout, "Hey, Piersall, you're nuts," or "You're still crazy, Piersall." Sometimes I'd ignore it. Other times I'd shout back something like "Kiss me!" and give him a big smile or maybe "Where's your wife, pal? One of our ball players is missing." Or something else equally raunchy. But as a matter of fact, the guys who yelled that kind of stuff at me did not really upset me. Sure, they were trying to get to me, but at the time I was more concerned with just playing ball. Some of the players, after a while, gave me a hard time but in fun. Willard Nixon, I remember, used to call me "Gooney." One guy who really used to give it to me was Dick Williams. That was a little later, around 1956 or '57, when he was with the Baltimore Orioles. He used to sit in the dugout and sing out, "Cuckoo, cuckoo, cuckoo." It used to make me laugh the way he'd say it, very high-pitched and drawn out, like "Coooo-coooo, coooo-coooo." I got a kick out of him.

From a baseball standpoint, it was a very good year for me. I had the right field job nailed down, and I was hitting well. But fielding was where I got the most notice. And after a little while, the sportswriters stopped wondering about whether I'd make it back. I got a lot of good press, and some people I respected said some very nice things about the way I was playing. Tris Speaker, for example, one of the game's all-time great outfielders, was quoted in one paper as saying about me, "He's a throwback to the old days when all outfielders could cover a piece of ground and throw and hit and do everything. He's going to be one of the great ones."

And Casey Stengel, who was managing the Yankees that year, was quoted by AP after one of our games against them that year in regard to my fielding: "Piersall is the best I've seen, and I've seen lots of them. [Tommy] Henrich was good, but he couldn't run with Piersall, and he couldn't get to those balls that Piersall catches. . . . That boy can do everything, and he makes it look easy. He throws you out at the plate, he doesn't let you go from first to third, he backs up the infield, and if you hit the ball over his head, he simply outruns the ball. He's an infielder and two outfielders rolled into one. . . . Mind you, I'm not saying Piersall is the greatest defensive outfielder I ever saw. . . . I watched some pretty fair country center fielders like Joe DiMaggio, Terry Moore, Jigger Statz. But right field? I've got to go with Piersall."

Curt Gowdy, our broadcaster in Boston that year, was also a big booster. He said in a magazine interview, "If you had to tally all the runs Piersall has saved the Red Sox this year with his spectacular fielding, you'd need an adding machine. In all my baseball experience, of the five best catches I've seen made, Piersall's made three of them."

For a guy who was trying to come back and who was worried about making it, these kinds of statements from guys of this caliber were really wonderful, and they helped more than I can say.

There were some really memorable moments that year. The one I like best happened during a game in Cleveland. Before it started I trotted by the Indians' bench and hollered, "Dig them crazy Indians." A couple of players shouted back. One of them said, "Come over here, Jimmy, and let us take the birdie off your head." Then they rode me pretty hard from the bullpen out in right field during most of the game.

One of the most vocal was Bob Lemon; he was really giving it to me. Well, in the ninth inning we were up 7–5. But we almost lost it. Wally Westlake walked for the Indians to lead it off. Then Al Rosen hit a little blooper to right that everyone thought was going to drop in for a hit. But I got a good jump on it, raced in, and got it about an inch off the ground. On the run, I threw to Dick Gernert, and we doubled Westlake off first. Then Billy Glynn

17

doubled, and Larry Doby drew a walk. We brought in Ellis Kinder to pitch, and they sent Bob Lemon up to pinch-hit.

Lemon is, of course, a Hall of Fame pitcher, but he was also a damn good hitter. He'd started out as a third baseman in the minors. I mean he hit 37 home runs in his career. And almost 38! Almost, because that afternoon he got hold of one that looked like it was going over the right field fence, but I got to it, leaped up, and grabbed it. It was the final out, and I ran with the ball over past the bullpen and waved it at all of them in it. "Eat your hearts out," I yelled. They didn't have a word to say. It was wonderful. After the game Larry Doby had a line I liked: "Never saw anybody better. He may be crazy but not in the outfield."

Lou Boudreau said to the reporters after the game that it was the best single inning he'd ever seen played by an outfielder. But the one comment that meant the most to me came from Bill McKechnie, whom I admired so much as a human being and as a coach. He seldom complimented anybody, and I mean anybody. But after the game he said, "Son, I never saw anybody play right field any better." I was so pleased I wanted to cry.

The same night the Cleveland Browns football offices, which were also in Municipal Stadium there, were broken into and robbed of $40,000. The next day there was an article about it in the *Cleveland Plain Dealer* in the sports section near the article about the game. The headline was "Browns Offices Robbed—Piersall Didn't Do It."

Another day I hit an inside-the-park home run against the Yankees. We were playing at Yankee Stadium, and Whitey Ford was pitching. I hit a line drive to center field, Mickey Mantle came charging in, and the ball went right by him. It went all the way to the 460-foot mark.

Then, in another game against the St. Louis Browns, I went six for six, the first time a Red Sox player ever did that in a nine-inning game. I remember I was five for five, and my final time up I looked down at Bob Elliott, who was playing third for them then. He'd been around a long time and had been a star with the Boston Braves for most of it. He looked at me and then moved back. I bunted and beat it out for my sixth hit. Thanks, Bob Elliott.

It was a Boston record. But the same day Ted Williams went zero for five, and the next day in the sports pages there was a little piece about my going six for six and a really big piece about Williams' not getting a hit in five times at bat. I think it was the first time he'd gone zero for five all year and maybe the second time in his life.

I got a two-base bunt that year, too. It was against the Yankees. I laid it down, and they watched it roll down the third baseline, waiting for it to go foul. Well, it just kept rolling straight, so I just kept going. Instead of running straight, I made the turn while they were still watching the ball. It rolled on past the third base bag, and I ended up on second with a bunt double. I don't think anybody's gotten a double out of a bunt since.

There were a few things that year that I would just as soon not remember. The foremost happened in a game with the St. Louis Browns. I hit a double off the wall. After sliding in, I got up and dusted myself off, and then Billy Hunter, their rookie shortstop, asked me to step off the base and kick the bag into line. I looked over at the umpire, Charlie Berry, and I got the feeling it was all right. So I stepped off the base, and Hunter, who had the ball hidden in his glove, tagged me out. That was the most embarrassing play of my life.

When I got back to our dugout, I said to Sid Hudson, who was pitching for us that game, that he had to do something with that guy for me. Well, his next time up, Hunter got a double himself, and before the first pitch to the next batter Hudson picked him off. That took some of the embarrassment away. But let me tell you, I never kicked a bag again for anybody.

I also accidentally broke a couple of Billy Goodman's

ribs that year. Goodman went after the umpire, Jim Duffy, about a call. I'd never seen him so mad. He was totally enraged. I thought he was going to slug Duffy, so I grabbed him from behind and pulled him away. I just wanted to keep him from doing something he'd be sorry for later. I dragged him all the way back to the dugout, and he kind of collapsed there. Later they took him to the hospital and found he had a couple of broken ribs. I guess I was stronger than I thought I was. "Overzealous" is the way one reporter put it.

In another game, this one against the Philadelphia As, I slid into second base headfirst, and there was a little stone that tore a helluva hole in my leg. The press wrote it up that I spiked myself, but that was wrong. How the hell could I spike myself in the thigh?

I really felt bad about it because I was out trying to stretch the hit into a double—it was the last out of the inning, and Ted Williams was on deck. It was even more embarrassing because we'd been told *not* to hit doubles if Williams was up next because then they'd walk Ted. The people came out to see Ted hit, not get walked. So I shouldn't have tried for second in the first place.

Anyway, they took me to the hospital and into the operating room. But there was a small portable radio there, and I wouldn't let them do anything to the leg until the game was over. We sat there—the doctor, the nurses, and I—and listened to the end of the game. Williams hit a home run, and we finally won it. Then I let them clean up the wound and stitch it up. I apologized to Ted the next day, too.

All in all, I had a really good year. Most of the writing was about my comeback and my fielding, but I hit .272 and drove in 52 runs, too. But best of all, my doubts about making it back and being accepted were washed away forever.

I don't know why they ever picked him [Anthony Perkins] to play me. I mean he threw a baseball like a girl, and he couldn't catch one with a bushel basket. He danced around the outfield like a ballerina, and he was supposed to be depicting me, a major league baseball player. I hated the movie.

2
GOOD TIMES
IN BOSTON

As a kid, I often dreamed of playing in an All-Star game. I always voted, especially for Ted Williams and Bobby Doerr of the Boston Red Sox, who were my biggest heroes when I was growing up. Well, in 1954, *my* dream came true.

I got more than 800,000 votes in the balloting that year, but I lost out to Hank Bauer of the Yankees, who was having a superb year. However, Casey Stengel, the manager of the American League All-Star team, picked me as an at-large player. I was chosen as a right fielder because that's the position I had started out at in the 1954 season, although I moved over to center field later. Tommy Umphlett, our center fielder the year before, was gone in 1954, and we had acquired Jackie Jensen from the Senators. He ended up in right field for us, and, of course, Ted Williams was in left. Ted and I were the only two Red Sox players to go to the All-Star game that year.

I was able to bring my father to the game, which was

23

very important to me. And the people at the *Boston Globe* asked me to write a column about the game. Actually, I had a ghostwriter, but I gathered all the information and gave him what I wanted him to write.

I was so honored just to be in the dugout that day with all the greatest players in the game that it didn't matter to me that I was not starting. Everybody was excited. I remember Mickey Vernon especially. He had brought along a camera, and he gave it to me and asked me to take pictures of him while he was playing first base during the game.

And I remember Ted Williams in the dugout, sitting there next to Al Rosen of the Indians, who was in the midst of a helluva batting slump. They were talking about it, and Williams told him that he needed to choke up on the bat a little, concentrate on being quicker with his hands and wrists, and stop trying to muscle the ball. The advice went something like that. And I'll be a son of a gun if Rosen didn't go out and hit two home runs in that game after their talk.

I didn't get into the game until the ninth inning. Minnie Minoso had been playing right field, and just before we took the field in the ninth he said to Casey, "Hey, put 'Leather' in." (That's a nickname Minoso had for me in those days.) Minnie said it, for one thing, because he wanted to see me play, not just come to the game and watch it from the dugout. But he had another reason. The sun was incredibly bright out there that afternoon, and he wanted out of the game because he didn't think he could catch a fly ball if one was hit to him.

Well, Casey did put me in for him. I went out there, and the first batter that inning for the National League was Duke Snider, who then hit three long foul balls to right. I honestly could not see them very well, and it really made me nervous. I was worried about screwing up if a fly ball came out my way and stayed fair. Then Duke hit one fair, which I lost for a moment in the sun but then managed to get under and catch. First I was relieved, and then I felt like I'd just hit a home run. Ted Kluszewski also hit a fly to right, and I caught that, too. Then Stan Musial flied out to left, and that was the ball game.

I didn't get a chance to bat in the game, but we won it 11–9 in what was then the highest-scoring All-Star game in baseball history. And it was the first time in five years that the American League had won. We scored three runs in the eighth to take it. Larry Doby pinch-hit a home run, and then Nellie Fox drove in another two runs with a single.

In another game that year, I learned a good lesson. We were playing Detroit and were leading 6–2 in the top of the ninth. I was on third base, and the Tigers' pitcher wasn't paying much attention to me. So I stole home. Everybody on the Detroit bench got on me. They were shouting "Bush," calling me a bush-leaguer for doing that when we had a four-run lead. One guy told me that wasn't good baseball. The hell it wasn't. Detroit got four runs in the bottom of the ninth, and we just escaped with a 7–6 win.

Mickey Owen came on with the Red Sox for a while in 1954. He was the catcher who committed the famous passed ball for the Brooklyn Dodgers in the ninth inning of Game 4 of the 1941 World Series and cost Brooklyn the game. Well, Mickey was 38 in 1954, but we needed a backup catcher. He'd been managing a team in the minor leagues in Norfolk, and the story was that he had gotten into some trouble. Seems he'd gotten into a fight with a fan who had come out of the stands and during it had bitten the guy's ear off. With this story preceding his arrival, none of us knew what he was going to be like. We were all a little leery, you might say. Anyway, he proved to be just a helluva nice guy. It turned out to be his last year in the major leagues, but he did hit a grand slam homer, and he said it was one of his greatest thrills in baseball.

I had a really good year in 1954. I was batting near .300

for most of it, but then I hurt my shoulder so badly that it would bother me for the rest of my career.

We were playing this exhibition game in Boston with the New York Giants for the "Jimmy Fund," which was a benefit for a children's hospital in Boston. As part of the hype for the game, they scheduled a pregame throwing contest between Willie Mays and me. I remember that a writer from one of the Boston papers referred to Mays as "a Piersall who hits home runs." I thought that was a very nice compliment. He got some other kinds of hits too, I might add, because he batted .345 that year, the best in the major leagues.

Well, we threw from all over the outfield, and we really went at it. I forget how many throws we made, but it was a lot, and I don't think there was a winner. I believe the judges said it was even. Unfortunately, my throwing arm really got a workout before the game. Late in the game, it was raining—a drizzle, not enough to call it off, but still it was coming down. Lou Boudreau, our manager, had taken all the other starters out of the game, but for some stupid reason he still had me in there. Shortly afterward, I made a strong throw and felt something tear in my shoulder. I could feel it all the way up into my neck.

There was a lot of speculation that I would be out for the rest of the season. I did get back into the lineup, however, but I was in a lot of pain. And my arm never did get back to normal. I ended up going to my own doctor to get cortisone shots, and I never told anybody in the Red Sox organization about it. For the next 13 years I had arm trouble. To compensate for it, I played shallower than I had before, and I taught myself to throw like a catcher to take some of the strain and pressure off my arm. All through the off-season between 1954 and 1955, I practiced throwing against a brick wall in my basement.

Despite the arm problem, I ended up with a .285 average, and only Ted Williams, who hit .345 until he was sidelined with a broken bone in his shoulder, and Billy Goodman, who hit .303, had better averages than me on the ball club that year. The Boston sportswriters voted me the Red Sox Most Valuable Player when the season was over, and I considered that quite an honor. As part of it, I got a Nash Rambler. It was such a boxy little car, I remember. One night the following winter I was driving to Providence, Rhode Island, to give a talk. The road was icy, and the Nash tipped over. I thought afterward that it was ironic, but the MVP award almost cost me my life.

The Red Sox didn't get to the World Series in 1954, but I did. I covered it for the *Boston Globe* with my ghostwriter. The other writers looked at me like "What the hell does he know about writing baseball?" Well, all of them were picking the Cleveland Indians to win it. In my first column before the series started, I said the New York Giants would win it in five games or less. They won it in four straight.

That was the Series in which Willie Mays made his famous back-to-the-infield catch, one of the most beautiful fielding plays ever made. Vic Wertz hit a towering fly ball to center, one that looked like nobody could get to it, but Mays turned around and raced after it like an Olympic sprinter and caught it over his shoulder somewhere around 450 feet from home plate. It was also the Series in which Dusty Rhodes hit so well. He won one game with a pinch-hit home run in extra innings and then won another game with his bat.

I got another honor that year, too. The Boston Chamber of Commerce named me one of its 10 outstanding young men for the year. Two of the others were Bobby Kennedy and Leonard Bernstein—not bad company for a center fielder.

With the way things were going, on and off the field, I'd gotten all my confidence back. Nineteen fifty-two was long gone, and I didn't feel I had to worry anymore about proving I could still play ball.

THE TRUTH HURTS

The next year my book—*Fear Strikes Out*, which I did with Al Hirshberg—came out, and I got a lot of publicity as a result. I certainly got a lot more speaking engagements. I also had a pretty fair year on the field. I batted .283 and hit 13 home runs. That was the most homers I'd hit in a single season up to that time.

But it wasn't until 1956 that I got back to the All-Star game. There was a lot of ink around that time about our having the best outfield in baseball. And we were doing well. Williams was hitting .368 and Jensen .311 and I was batting .301. As it turned out, I was not going to start that year either. As a center fielder, I had to run against Mickey Mantle, who by the All-Star break already had hit 29 home runs. He was having some trouble with his knee but still would have a super year. He ended up winning the Triple Crown: .353 average, 52 home runs, and 130 RBIs. Then he hit three homers and drove in six runs in the World Series.

Casey Stengel again picked me for the American League team, and he almost started me as well, because he was worried about Mantle's knee, but finally he went with Mickey. I got in for the eighth and ninth innings, however, handled a fly ball hit by Hank Aaron, and in my one at-bat grounded out to shortstop.

There were a couple of other Red Sox on the All-Star team that year. Naturally, Ted Williams was one, and he hit a two-run homer in the game. Mickey Vernon was the starting first baseman, but he didn't do anything the fans could cheer about. And Tom Brewer pitched a couple of innings. The National League won it 7–3.

The game was played in Washington, and I brought my father down for it. My wife came, too. That was also the year they started to make the movie of *Fear Strikes Out*. Anthony Perkins was the movie star they picked to play me. He sent me a telegram just before the All-Star game, congratulating me on being selected to play in it. It also said: "Entire cast and crew of 'The Jim Piersall Story' will be rooting for you via television on stage six at Paramount Studios in Hollywood. Looking forward to meeting you in the near future. Good Luck. Sincerely Anthony Perkins."

I don't know why they ever picked him to play me. I mean he threw a baseball like a girl and he couldn't catch one with a bushel basket. He danced around the outfield like a ballerina, and he was supposed to be depicting me, a major league baseball player. I hated the movie. What made it even more ridiculous was the fact that Perkins was left-handed and I was right-handed. So the director said that they had to teach him to throw right-handed. So what did they do to accomplish that? They hired Tommy Holmes, who had played in the outfield for the Boston Braves during the 1940s, to teach him. The only problem was that Holmes himself threw and batted left-handed. It was a joke. If you thought Perkins looked silly throwing the ball left-handed, you should have seen him flit it with his right hand.

It wasn't Tony Perkins's fault that he wasn't an athlete. I mean he is a brilliant actor and a very intelligent guy. I met him when we appeared together on the "Ed Sullivan Show" to promote the movie, and I liked him a lot. In fact, a movie he made a couple of years after that, *Psycho*, in which he plays the role of a real weirdo, is one of my favorite movies.

As I mentioned, I didn't like the movie *Fear Strikes Out*. It was a lot of bullshit, just a heap of fiction. One thing that particularly galled me was an incredible thing that occurred one night at Fenway Park. The film crew was there to get footage of the crowd, of the baseball game in action, stuff to be inserted into the movie to make it all look authentic. The real game action shots were supposed to feature me, shot at regular games. Well, anyway, the director said to me before the game, "See if you can hit a home run for us tonight, will you, Jimmy?"

I said jokingly, "Sure. Why not?"

THE TRUTH HURTS

Well, in the ninth inning, the score was tied at one run apiece. Dick Gernert got on base for us, and I was up. Jack Harshman was pitching for the White Sox, and he had given us a lot of trouble for a long time. He threw a fastball to me with the count two and nothing, and I'll be damned if I didn't hit it out of the ballpark. I wasn't sure it was going to make it, but then as I was running I saw Harshman start to walk off the mound, his head down, and I knew it was out of there. A storybook ending, and they got it all on film—the hit, me running, Harshman walking dejectedly off the field, the crowd on its feet cheering, the whole thing—and then they never used it.

Earlier in that game, I made one of the better catches of my career, robbing Sherm Lollar of an extra-base hit. Of course, they didn't use that either.

Instead, they made up all kinds of crap. Things that never happened. Things that were not even in the book. The whole movie story was dreamed up in Hollywood. I never climbed any screen. And that was a big thing in the movie, supposed to be very dramatic. Hell, it never happened. And they had the relationship between my father and me dead wrong. Karl Malden played my father, and he did a wonderful job—of acting, anyway. All his mannerisms reminded me of my father; he really had the part down. But he was playing a role that was essentially wrong. He played it just as it was written by the screenwriters. They made my father out to be a real bastard, one who was trying to drive me to a mental breakdown. Well, he wasn't. I have never blamed my father for that breakdown. My father and I actually had a good relationship.

They also had him coming to visit me in the sanitarium. He never did that. He wasn't supposed to, according to the doctors. But that's the way they showed it. The whole movie was filled with things that simply had not happened in my life.

When the movie came out, I took one look at it and said,

30

"horseshit." It was not about the Jimmy Piersall I knew.

After the All-Star game, I continued to hit pretty well in 1956. I was up around .300 most of the time although I had a slump in August and dropped down to about .290. Some of my fans from Waterbury and Bridgeport, Connecticut, got together and arranged with the ball club to have a Jimmy Piersall Day. It was set for September 22nd, and I was really touched by it. When the day came, I'd gotten my batting average back up to .299. And I'd scored 90 runs and gotten 169 hits, including 38 doubles, all of those stats the highest on the Red Sox at the time.

My wife came to the game and the ceremony with three of our little girls, the ones who were three, four, and five at the time. My father was there in a box behind home plate. The mayor of Waterbury gave me a certificate. They gave me all kinds of presents: savings bonds for my kids, a wristwatch, a crib for my four-month-old, just all kinds of things.

I gave a little thank-you speech, and then we went out and lost to the Yankees 2–1. I didn't get a hit in four at-bats. I guess you can't have everything in one day. The New York pitcher, whom I couldn't buy a hit from that day, was Don Larsen, the guy who two weeks later would pitch a perfect game in the World Series.

When the season ended I had played in all 156 games, hadn't missed a single one. My average dropped to .293, although that was still the highest in my career up to that time. I ended with 40 doubles, and that was the most any player had made in either league in 1956. I got 176 hits, second best on the Red Sox, six less than Jackie Jensen got. And I scored 91 runs, as did Billy Klaus, our third baseman—the most anyone on the team made.

I felt very good about the year. And I felt even better when the Boston chapter of the Baseball Writers of America named me the Red Sox MVP.

The next year the movie came out, and there was a lot of

press about it. It actually got good reviews and was a success at the box office, even though it was not a true portrayal. Needless to say, the publicity helped me. There were even rumors that I was going to be signed to a Hollywood contract myself. Louella Parsons wrote that I was going to star in a movie called *Clarence,* which was a comedy by Booth Tarkington. Well, if Anthony Perkins could play me, why not? But it never came about.

I held out for more money in 1957. I felt I deserved it after the good year I'd had in '56. I was asking for $25,000 for the year, which was $7,500 more than I'd gotten the year before. I finally signed for $22,500. Today, somebody who hit .293 batting lead-off, led both leagues in doubles, won the Golden Glove Award, and led both leagues in fielding would earn $700,000 a year easy.

We ended up third in 1957, behind the Yankees and the White Sox, 16 games out of first. I didn't have as good a year as I'd had in '56, but I did hit 19 home runs, the most I would ever hit in a single season. And I scored the most runs on the Red Sox, 103, and stole the most bases, 14. I batted .261.

There weren't any honors that year—except one. Gussie Moran, the tennis player who used to wear those frilly, lacy panties when she played, had a piece in *Sport* magazine in which she picked the 10 most handsome men in baseball. I was one of them. The whole thing was a big laugh. She said, "There is great depth in his face. If I were an artist with a brush, this is the man I'd like to paint."

The other nine lucky devils, along with Gussie's comments were: Eddie Mathews, "a spoiled cherub look, the Tyrone Power of baseball"; Vinegar Bend Mizell, "a backwoods species, each girl watching wishes she was his Daisy Mae"; Ray Boone, "somebody's big brother, but no girl in her right mind would want to feel platonic about him"; Robin Roberts, "a born leader, fit for a position in government"; Bob Friend, "a girl's first crush, the fellow who used to carry your books home from school"; Jerry Coleman, "a fashion plate even when he's making an error"; Bobby Avila, "a Rudolph Valentino, he makes you think of moonlight nights south of the border"; Gino Cimoli, "pretty, with long lashes, but he's all man"; and Gus Bell, "the boy you want to invite to the junior prom." I'd rather have made the All-Star team.

I didn't get to the All-Star game in 1958 either, for pretty valid reasons. I was not having a good year because I got hurt. As a result, I was not hitting the ball anywhere near like I had the three or four years before.

What happened was that Billy Martin, who was with the Detroit Tigers that year, got me as I was sliding into second base one game. He landed on me with his knees as I was trying to break up a double play. It was not done on purpose by any means, but he came down hard and broke a rib of mine. I eventually got back into the lineup, but I was really hurting. I'd been hitting around .275 before the injury, but after I came back it was truly painful to bat—and my average showed it. I really shouldn't have been playing at all. But the Red Sox weren't doing very well at the time, and Pinky Higgins said he wanted me in there at least for my fielding, which I could handle without a whole lot of trouble. It was, unfortunately, terribly uncomfortable. Anyone who has broken a rib or torn a ribcage knows how painful it can be and how long it takes to heal.

Luckily, my fielding wasn't affected at all. In fact, the *Sporting News* conducted a poll of the players in each league to pick All-Star fielding teams. I felt honored to be chosen as the American League center fielder, especially because the selection was made by my fellow ball players. The other players on our All-Star fielding team were Vic Power at first, Frank Bolling at second, Frank Malzone at third, Luis Aparicio at shortstop, Norm Siebern in left, Al Kaline in right, and Sherm Lollar behind the plate.

Because of the 1958 rib injury I played in only 125

games. When the season was over, I had an average of just .237, by far my worst in the eight years I'd been playing major league baseball. In one year, I'd gone from 103 runs to 55, from 159 hits to just 99, from 19 home runs to eight.

There had been rumors about my being traded after the 1957 season; there always seemed to be talk about that in regard to me. I never put much stock in it, but after the 1958 season finally and mercifully came to an end, I began to think a little bit about the possibility.

I was only 28 years old then, and I knew I was not slowing down. But the poor stats did make me worry. With good cause, as I would shortly find out.

Joe Cronin looked across his desk at me and said, "No, Jimmy, we're not going to trade you. Everything's okay here. Don't worry about it." So I didn't worry about it. I started my own food brokerage business, called it Jimmy Piersall Inc., bought the house, and then a few weeks later Cronin traded me to Cleveland.

3
IN CLEVELAND

Nothing good ever happens on December 7th. I found that out in 1958. That was the day Arthur Siegel, one of the Boston sportswriters, called to tell me that I'd just been traded to Cleveland for Vic Wertz and Gary Geiger. I was stunned, really thunderstruck—for a very good reason, as I'll explain. My next reaction was simply not to believe him. After all, nobody from the Red Sox had contacted me about any trade. I hadn't heard a thing from the front office or from our manager, Pinky Higgins.

But it was true.

The reason I was so surprised, so unwilling to believe it, was because of what had taken place about a month earlier. I had gone to see our general manager, Joe Cronin, who had been so helpful to me back in 1952. I told Joe that I had something very important to talk to him about. And it was that very topic—being traded or, more precisely, *not* being traded.

That season, 1958, hadn't been one of my best because

of playing with a broken rib most of the year. But prior to that I'd had five straight good years, which I assumed counted for something.

So I sat down with Cronin. I said I wanted to know if there was any chance I might be traded. The reason I wanted to know—needed to know, I explained to him—was that I was planning to go into business for myself in Boston and would be investing $16,000 of my own money in it. I also was thinking about buying a bigger house; we'd found one with 18 rooms, which, back then, I could buy for $23,500. At that time we had six kids, ranging in age from seven to one, and we had another on the way. I sure didn't want to launch a business and commit to a big house if I was going to be traded. For me, those were two pretty hefty investments.

Joe Cronin looked across his desk at me and said, "No, Jimmy, we're not going to trade you. Everything's okay here. Don't worry about it."

So I didn't worry about it. I started my own food brokerage business, called it Jimmy Piersall Inc., bought the house, and then a few weeks later Cronin traded me to Cleveland. Cronin didn't even call me to tell me. Boy, that really pissed me off. He didn't have enough guts to tell me himself. Nobody in the organization told me. Not a single word from Cronin, who featured himself as a smooth politician, a diplomat, but in the end proved that he was really nothing more than a con artist.

I had wanted to stay in Boston. I understood, of course, that trades were all part of the game. That's why I went to Cronin in the first place. But I really liked Boston. I had loyal fans there who treated me wonderfully in those days. I used to get standing ovations when I'd make a good catch or get a key hit. I was very lucky to be playing there in those years, very fortunate because the fans had built up my name, which helped me not only in my profession but also in off-season jobs.

IN CLEVELAND

Security was very important to me then. I had never had a lot of money. Before baseball I'd worked in a silver factory, unloaded freight cars, driven a plow, refereed high school basketball games. Crummy jobs, and I hated them.

So when I got to Boston and into the big leagues I wanted to get some kind of financial security for myself besides baseball. After all, major league baseball didn't pay all that much back then, and it was hardly the most secure job in the world.

I worked hard in the off-season. I worked my way up in the business world by promoting food products, first for Colonial Provision Company and then for the John E. Cain Food Company. By 1958, I was earning $25,000 a year in the off-season. That was more money than I made as a ball player; in fact, my top salary with the Red Sox was only $22,500, and in the first few years I made like $5,000 one year and $7,000 the next. But by 1958, I was doing real well, and that's why I decided to invest in my own company, because I knew by that time that it would be a success if I was *there*, in Boston, to promote it myself. Of course, as it turned out, I wasn't, and it didn't go. As a result, I had to get out of the business shortly afterward, and I ended up losing about $12,000.

Frank Lane was the general manager at Cleveland in 1959. We talked after the trade, and he told me that the Indians were a real first-class operation, that everything was done first-rate, and that I would really like it there. I liked Lane very much and thought he was always fair with everybody. But I can't say the same for his manager that year, Joe Gordon. He and I never got along, but then he didn't get along with too many people.

I joined the Cleveland ball club at spring training in Tucson, Arizona. We were supposed to stay at the Santa Rita Hotel. When I got there the first guy I bumped into in the lobby was Billy Martin. Lane had also traded for him that year, and he too had just arrived. We went up to our rooms, which, as it turned out, were right next to each other, and I'll be a son of a buck if we both didn't find huge cockroaches in them. So we gathered them up. Billy took his, I took mine, and we went downstairs and dropped them on the front desk. The lady there fainted.

We bitched to Frank Lane about it. "A real first-class act," we said. "Nothing but the best with Cleveland, and here we are staying in Cockroach Manor." Finally, to get us off his back, Lane took Billy and me to a cowboy store out there and bought us hats and belts and boots, all kinds of western clothes. It must have cost him four hundred bucks to pacify us. That was my introduction to the Cleveland ball club—cockroaches.

We had a fine baseball team there and some very nice guys. Besides Billy Martin, there was Vic Power, who became a good friend of mine, and Woodie Held, our shortstop. I was in the outfield with Rocky Colavito, who led the American League that year with 42 home runs, and Minnie Minoso, who was 36 but still batted .302. There were a couple of other old-timers there, too: Elmer Valo, who was 38, and Mike Garcia, who was Minoso's age.

Minoso was Frank Lane's "Bobo" (that was a piece of baseball slang we used for "favorite" in those days). For some reason or other, Lane bought Minoso a pink Cadillac convertible. The first day he had it we were playing the Yankees in Cleveland and there were about 60,000 people in Municipal Stadium. Well, at one point in the game while we were out in the field it started to rain. The umpires didn't stop it because it wasn't coming down that hard, but Minoso ran off the field and into the dugout. Everyone just stood there and watched him. Minnie did not speak English very well, and he was jumping up and down in the dugout, shouting, "Up top down! Up top down!" No one knew what the hell he was talking about. But he kept yelling that until somebody finally figured it out and sent the clubhouse boy out to put the top to his convertible up. Then Minnie trotted back out onto the field and we resumed the game.

We had Mudcat Grant on our pitching staff that year. He was young; it was only his second year in the majors. He had a good year, as I recall, but he got his ass in a sling, too. I was out in the bullpen one game when it happened. I hadn't been having a very good year, so they were playing Tito Francona in center field. He had a marvelous year— batted .363 and hit 20 homers. They had me in the bullpen so I could yell to him where to play the different batters. Anyway, we were standing there during the national anthem this particular day, and when we came to the end of it Mudcat sang "land of the free, *my ass!*" Well, we had this pitching coach who was from the South and was not all that wild about blacks in the first place, and when he heard it he really blew his stack. He reamed Mudcat up and down. Then he went to Frank Lane about it, who in turn suspended Mudcat without pay for something like a month. Mudcat was not a bad guy, but he made a big mistake that day.

I didn't have a good year in 1959, hit only .246, but the team did well. We gave the White Sox a run for the pennant and finished second, five games out.

The next year was a different story, however. The team didn't do all that well, fourth place and not even a .500 season, but I had a very good year. At the All-Star break I was hitting something like .340 and had maybe 10 home runs and 45 RBIs. I was right up there at the very top of the league. Even so, Paul Richards, the Baltimore manager, who was managing the American League All-Stars, didn't pick me. I was really pissed because I felt I deserved to be on the All-Star team. It was really unfair.

At the beginning of the year, however, I didn't even know if I was going to start. They moved me to right field because Harvey Kuenn had gotten hurt. Joe Gordon was playing this big rookie, a kid named Walt Bond, in center field. He did well in spring training: hit some home runs and looked pretty good all around. But when the regular season started he went something like 1 for 40 and was batting maybe .025. Then he came up to me and said, "You're telling the opposition how to pitch to me." I couldn't believe it; he really thought I was telling the opposing pitchers how to pitch to him. Well, that was one of the craziest things I ever heard. I laughed at him and said, "Jeez, if I thought of it, I would've done it!" It didn't matter. I was hitting the ball real well and he wasn't, so Gordon put me back in center field and put Bond on the bench.

I had several run-ins with the White Sox that year. I remember one day when we were playing a doubleheader in Chicago. I had a 15-game hitting streak going, and I was really hot to keep it going. Well, in the first game I got on base with a fielder's choice and then stole second base. Early Wynn was pitching for the White Sox, and he used to get away with a lot of high sliders. He was pitching to Harvey Kuenn, whom Lane had acquired from the Tigers before the season, and Larry Napp was umpiring behind the plate. The first pitch was high, but Napp called it a strike.

"Hey, that's too high." I yelled. "What're you doing, Napp?"

The second base umpire, a rookie by the name of Cal Drummond, came over to me and said, "Knock it off."

"I'm not talking to you," I said.

The next pitch was also a little high, and Napp gave him another strike. So I shouted at Napp again, "That's too damn high. Jesus, can't you see that for yourself?"

Well, over comes Drummond. "I told you to shut up before," he said.

"And I told you before I wasn't talking to you."

IN CLEVELAND

"You'd better shut up, or I'm going to throw you out of the game."

That's when I said, "Oh, fuck me." And he threw me out of the game. Well, I went bananas. I mean I really blew up. There went my 15-game hitting streak. I was truly pissed. I went over to our dugout and started throwing everything I could get my hands on out onto the field: bats, balls, everything. Then I walked across the infield to the White Sox dugout, which you had to pass through to get to your dressing room back then. Well, the fans were going wild by this time and when I got over there, Jim Rivera, their right fielder, was laughing like hell. He handed me a pail of sand, and I threw it out onto the field. Then he handed me a bucket of garbage, and out it went; then a pail of orange peels, which I tossed out, too.

Up in the clubhouse, the doctor tried to get me to take a tranquilizer, but I wouldn't. I got myself calmed down without his help, and I was back in the lineup for the second game.

Then I had my second incident of the day. Bill Veeck, the White Sox owner, had his new scoreboard that year out behind center field—the "banshee board" they call it. It was the one where all kinds of fireworks and sirens would go off if a White Sox player hit a home run or after a Sox win or some such crap. God, it was loud. All kinds of junk, the debris from the firecrackers, would come floating down on you in center field after it went off. It also stunk like hell from the gunpowder in all the fireworks.

Well, I caught the last out of the game, a long fly to center. But just after I did I was hit on the ear by an orange thrown by somebody in the stands. It hurt like hell, so I turned around and threw the baseball I had as far as I could at the scoreboard, and that was a helluva distance. It went way the hell up and hit Veeck's precious scoreboard and caused some kind of short circuit. Was Veeck furious!

43

THE TRUTH HURTS

The next day the *Chicago Tribune* ran the headline: "Piersall Hit Veeck Where It Hurts Most—Scoreboard." Well, Veeck ranted and raved about it for days—"that damn Piersall trying to wreck my scoreboard." He got a lot of mileage out of it with the press, and he loved that. Everybody was talking about his beloved scoreboard and how I'd tried to ruin it for him. I wish I had broken his damn scoreboard; it was such a pain in the ass.

Another incident that year got a lot of attention from the press. We were playing the Tigers in Detroit. Pete Burnside was pitching for them. Early in the game I hit a two-run homer into the upper deck, and as I was going around the bases I stopped at third and doffed my cap at the Detroit dugout, to the players who had been giving me an especially hard time earlier. It was, incidentally, the longest home run of my career, about 430 feet. A couple of innings later I came up again. Well, I brought out a batting helmet this time, the kind they use today. Only in 1960 nobody wore one. I did it because Frank Lane thought they were good for the players and that someone ought to test them out. I mean break the tradition. Also I thought Burnside was probably going to throw at me.

Well, I got up there with the helmet on, and the Tiger catcher, Red Wilson, went bananas. He said all kinds of things to me, baiting me, and he told Burnside to throw at me. And Burnside did throw at me. The first pitch brushed me back, and I had to jump out of the way. The next pitch was even closer. The third pitch was *behind* me. With that, the umpire, John Flaherty, went out and told him to stop throwing at me. It cost Burnside a $50 fine.

All the time, Wilson was ranting at me. I turned to him and said, "You know, where I was, there were a lot of people locked up, and you're crazier than all of them." He looked at me for a second and then broke up laughing. I was calm as hell that day. I enjoyed getting to them, though, and I really did that day. The writers were all on my side after that episode. It was a nice change.

Those weren't the only problems that year. In 1960, I got thrown out of some other ball games, and suddenly the whole thing got blown into a major event.

You see, my family was living back in Boston that year. The kids were young and growing, and I felt it wasn't fair to them to keep moving them around. So they stayed in the big house I'd bought there. But often during the season I'd try to get home Sunday on a six o'clock flight from Cleveland. In those days, we'd play a doubleheader on Sunday and then have Monday off. Most of the time I couldn't make it because the six o'clock flight was the last of the day.

This particular Sunday we were playing the Yankees, and early in the second game I tried to steal second base. Hank Soar was the umpire at second. I slid in and beat the throw easily, I thought. Soar called me out. I couldn't believe it and jumped up. I really argued with him because I was sure I was safe. He wasn't so sure, and he threw me out of the game. Well, this definitely gave me a chance to catch the six o'clock flight. But it stirred up a lot in the press box, a lot of questions about getting thrown out and then going home. Then somebody from the Cleveland front office said he thought I deliberately got thrown out of the game so I could catch the last plane home.

So, when I got off the plane in Boston, there were TV cameras, media people, reporters, all waiting for me. Not only had the Cleveland front office hinted that I got myself thrown out on purpose, but they had leaked word to the wire services that Frank Lane and Joe Gordon wanted me to see a psychiatrist. I couldn't believe that, especially of Gordon, because he had enough of his own problems because of his drinking and he needed a psychiatrist more than I did. But anyway, that's what they wanted, I was told.

So I decided to go to one. I found one in Boston. When I went to him I told him I wanted him to charge me $100 an hour. I said, "I won't talk to you unless you do. Charge the most you can because the Indians are paying for it and I feel the whole thing is very unfair to me."

I only saw him once. I explained to him that we were in a pennant race and that I was playing hard. Maybe I needed a rest, needed to sit on the bench for a while, but I didn't need a psychiatrist. I said to him that no one says anything when I make a great catch or save a ball game, but now, when I get thrown out of a couple of games, right away they say I'm not well and that I'm hurting the ball club. A sportswriter named Harry Jones of the *Cleveland Plain Dealer* did a story on that. He really went after me. I don't understand it, because the four games I'd gotten thrown out of we won anyway. To make a big thing out of it because of my previous problems with mental illness, I told the psychiatrist, I thought was dead wrong. I got thrown out of a game and they said I needed treatment. If somebody else had done it, they wouldn't have thought a thing about it. Well, the psychiatrist agreed with me, and after the first visit he called Frank Lane in Cleveland and told him he thought it would be better for me to go back with the team and maybe sit on the bench and rest for a couple of days. A little rest was all I needed. Lane sort of compromised and said that he wanted me to take a full week off. Well, I wasn't happy about it, but finally I just looked on it as a little vacation. They were paying me whether I sat on the bench in Cleveland or at my house back in Boston.

On the first day back we were playing the Chicago White Sox again, and I went three for five against Early Wynn. From then on I hit the ball pretty good, and I felt good about the way I was playing.

But it was still hard to convince everyone I wasn't about to crack at any moment. Umpires, for example, have come running up after I've protested some play, saying, "Look at his eyes. Look at his eyes. See if he's all right." I remember a perfect example of that kind of incident that happened the same year in Cleveland. We were playing the Yankees, and Jim Coates, a big, skinny, ugly right-hander, was pitching. He'd knock you down in a minute and think nothing about it. Well, Ted Williams taught guys like myself always to watch the pitcher throwing *before* you got up in the batter's box: watch how he's throwing while he's warming up, see how his breaking ball is breaking, that kind of thing.

So I was up by the batter's box, watching Coates while he was warming up. He saw me standing there staring at him. Then with his next warm-up he threw right at me. I was just standing there, out of the batter's box, with three bats. In those days, we didn't have donuts or that kind of thing; we simply took along a couple of extra bats for the weight. So anyway, when he threw at me, I leaped. Up went the bats and down I went. He almost hit me. So I yelled, "What the hell's going on here?" And he just stood out there on the mound, looking as if nothing happened. Well, I picked up the bats, walked a little toward the mound, and then threw all three bats. They went everywhere—one toward him, another down the line, everywhere. And then all four umpires ran up to me, and suddenly they were psychiatrists. "Look at his eyes," one of them said. "See if he's okay." Another one was looking into my eyes. "He's okay," he yelled.

I said, "I'm okay. Sure, I'm okay. It's him. He threw the ball at me, you dumb bastards. Go look in his eyes."

Another example was at another game in Cleveland that year, although I was the antagonist in this situation. We were playing against Boston, and Vic Power was our first baseman. He was the best defensive first baseman I ever saw. His reflexes were tremendous. He could make plays nobody else could. Anyway, at this particular game we had a full house, about 55,000 people. A guest of the ball club that day was Woody Hayes, the Ohio State football coach.

THE TRUTH HURTS

He was sitting in the box seats hollering at Vic, calling him a showboat. He was doing it mainly because Vic ordinarily caught a ball with one hand, even pop-ups. And Hayes was all over him for it. I knew what was going to happen because Vic had a real temper. In fact, we had a lot of tempers that year: Johnny Temple, myself, Woody Held, Vic. Finally Vic had had about as much as he would take and headed over to where Hayes was sitting—probably just to holler back, maybe tell him what he thought of loudmouth football coaches. As he did, the photographers, who were on the field in those days, also knew that something was up and started over after him. I knew if they got a picture of Vic shouting at Woody Hayes, or doing something worse, they'd crucify Vic in the paper the next day. So I took all three of them out with a block.

Everything cleared up quickly after that. But it wasn't over. The photographers had to get back by first base, and each inning I had to go by them to get to my position. Well, they weren't happy with me because of the block and told me about it. So after that, every inning, instead of trotting by them—they were down on a knee—I jumped over them. And as I did, I hollered or swore at them. They didn't like that either. The next day in the paper the sports editor wrote a column about me, ripping me up about everything he could think of, taking it right to my fan club, which then had about 5,000 members. He just tore me apart from one end of the column to the other. Really vicious. He said the girls and boys in the fan club should hear the language I used. That their parents should. That they shouldn't be my fans. Really panned me. It was so one-sided that even the Yankee players (who came into town that day to open a series) were mad about it. Bill Skowron was especially ticked off, and he told me so. And obviously I was hot. I mean this guy talked about my being immoral. Well, the fact of the matter was that he should have looked at some of his fellow sportswriters around that time if he was worried about morality, because half of them were the biggest drunks and freeloaders around. I swore, sure, but I didn't use the Lord's name, just a bunch of man-made words that were probably appropriate at the time.

The next day the father of the president of my fan club, who was, as it turned out, an editorial writer on the same paper, wrote an article that appeared smack on the editorial page, not in the sports section, in response to the other story, and he defended me. I thought that was one of the finest things ever to happen to me, to have somebody come to my defense like that on his own. He took the other side and told the positive things I'd done, all about the time and work I'd put in and the things I'd done to promote an understanding of mental health and about some of the people with mental problems whom I'd helped.

He also talked about some of the things I'd had to put up with when I came back, like guys coming onto the field after me, harassments, and some so-called fans who were the real nuts, like the ones who terrorized two of my kids one day outside the ballpark in Cleveland when they were waiting for me to come out. All my children were sitting in the car, and these guys were shouting, swearing at them, saying awful things about me. It scared them half to death. They were so upset. In fact, two of the little girls threw up in the car. I had to chase the jerks away with a baseball bat.

I encountered a lot of that kind of thing in my career because I was Jimmy Piersall and I'd had a mental problem. Sure, I brought a lot of the things on myself. I was high-strung. In those days, if I'd had lithium, as I do today, it would have been a different story. My chemical balance would have been a lot better. I know it's helped me since.

The three years I spent in Cleveland with the Indians were interesting and hectic ones. They were also good financially. I made more money there in three years than in all the years in Boston combined. I was representing a company called Neptune Sardines. I had big signs made up and then got some kids to hang them at the ballpark during the games. I'd give the television cameramen cases of sardines, and they'd focus on the signs whenever they got a chance. It was great free advertising.

The guys in the club got to like sardines, too. I used to bring cases of them into the clubhouse, and everybody would eat them, especially Tito Francona. He used to eat pounds of them at a sitting. His wife came up to me after a while and said, "Jimmy, don't give him any more of those sardines. He stinks up the whole house when he comes home." I guess we pretty well stunk up the Cleveland clubhouse too.

With my book out and selling well, the movie, and all the publicity, I was getting offers for public appearances right and left. I even made a record that year entitled "Please Jimmy Piersall, I'm a Rookie," with a trio of girls called the "Heartbreakers." God, it was terrible.

I was promoting all kinds of things, appearing every-where. During that time it wasn't out of the ordinary for me to make $800 on the side on a Saturday afternoon, and this was in the early '60s, when that was a lot of money.

Joe Gordon left later in the 1960 season. Whoopee! He went over to Detroit, but Rocky Colavito, a good friend of mine who'd played with me under Gordon and had been traded over there, sure as hell didn't say, "Whoopee." JoJo White, one of our coaches, took over for a game. He was one of the finest human beings I've known in my life. Actually, Gordon was traded for Jimmy Dykes—the only time, I think, in baseball history that a manager was traded for another manager. Leave it to Lane. Anyway, Dykes took over and called me into his office. He knew about most of the incidents I'd been involved in earlier in the season. "Jimmy," he said, "you're my center fielder. I like the way you play. But let's get one thing straight. I'll take care of the umpires." I said, "Okay." Later, when I would go after an umpire about something or other, I'd hear him bellow, "Jimmy, shut up!" It was loud, penetrating, and it worked. I'd just stop. I wished I'd had Dykes all my life.

Our general manager, Frank Lane, later went over to Kansas City. I would miss him. I didn't know how much until I had some awful dealings with the guy who replaced him, Gabe Paul.

Despite all the hectic events of the '60 season, I still had a good enough year. I hit .282, 18 home runs, stole 18 bases. And I was glad Gordon was gone and Jimmy Dykes was there.

The following year was great for me. But there was one sad incident—my father died. It happened at my house. He had a heart attack and died in my arms. I was away from the club for a few days until the funeral was over. Then, my first day back, which was in New York, two guys came running out of the stands after me. This was 1961, and Mantle and Maris were going for Babe Ruth's record of 60 home runs. Well, we were walking Maris every time he came to bat. There were about 60,000 people in Yankee Stadium that day, and they were getting a little annoyed. In the second game of the doubleheader, after we'd walked Maris for about the eighth time, these two guys came charging toward me in center field. I didn't know whether they had knives or razors or whether they were crazy or drunk. One of them was about 19 and the other maybe 21. One of them was shouting, "You crazy bastard, Piersall, we're going to get you." I decked the one that was shouting as soon as he got to me. Then the other one started to run away and I chased after him and kicked him in the ass. I kicked him so hard my toe was black and blue for a week. And then everybody was out there—my teammates, Mantle had run out to help me, the ground crew, the security guys, the police. And I think everybody got a shot at the punks. By the time they hauled them off the field, their faces looked like golf balls. But it had been pretty scary for a minute.

THE TRUTH HURTS

In 1961, I had my best year ever at the plate. I hit .322, fourth best in the American League. Only Norm Cash of the Tigers (.361), Elston Howard of the Yankees (.348), and Al Kaline of Detroit (.324) did any better. And what did I get for it? Traded.

After the 1960 season, my contract was up and I had to negotiate it with the owners because they hadn't hired a general manager to replace Frank Lane. Well, one of the provisions they put into it was that if I didn't get thrown out of a game during the season I'd get a $5,000 bonus.

By the end of the year, Gabe Paul was the general manager. I had gotten thrown out of a couple of games, but I talked with the owners about the incidents, and in each case they thought I'd been justified and shouldn't have been thrown out of the game. In light of that and the quality of my play that year, they agreed that I should still get the bonus.

After our final series out in Los Angeles, however, Gabe Paul asked me to come to his suite in the hotel we were staying at. He told me to sit down and then asked if I really thought I deserved the bonus money.

"You're damn right I deserve it," I said.

"Well, you know, you only drove in 40 runs all year," he said.

"Of course, I did. I was the lead-off batter for chrissake, hitting behind the pitcher, and somebody else who was probably batting .240. What the hell do you expect? You can't drive in runs if nobody is on base. I *scored* 81 runs. And I *batted* .322."

He told me he didn't think I honestly did well enough to warrant the bonus. He was implying that the bonus depended not only on not getting thrown out of games, but also on *his interpretation* of my performance.

Well, I was really mad. I told him that was not the deal and that I'd just talked it over with the owners, the ones with whom I made the deal initially. They felt that I'd earned it. I had it on their word.

Then he turned to me and asked out of the blue, "How do you feel about being traded?"

"That's up to you," I said.

"Well, I think you've been bad for the team's public relations. I don't think you're presenting the proper image to the fans. So I've talked with Eddie Doherty (the general manager of the Washington Senators) about a trade."

"I don't give a good goddam what you do," I said, "but give me the money that's owed to me."

At that, he went over and got an envelope and handed it to me. The money was in it. It just killed him to have to give it to me.

Then, in honor of my best season in the major leagues, he traded me to Washington.

Well, Casey [Stengel], by this time, was about 75 years old, and he used to fall asleep in the dugout about the fifth inning of every game. . . . Duke [Snider] looked at me and said, "Go get him." . . . so I went down to the end of the bench and back into the runway. . . . I hollered, "Hey!" real loud. And Casey jumped up and started giving signs to the ground crew.

4
OTHER TEAMS, OTHER TOWNS

After Cleveland, I was a real carpetbagger for the next two years. And, I can say frankly, a most unhappy one. I stayed with Washington for all of 1962, but I ended up with three different teams in 1963: the Senators, the Mets, and the Los Angeles Angels.

When I went to Washington I was looking for a big raise. I wanted a two-year contract at $50,000 a year. After all, I'd just come off the best year of my baseball career. Well, Ed Doherty, the general manager of the Senators, wouldn't give it to me. So I threatened to hold out, but it was a weak threat.

It was not easy for me to negotiate with Ed because I'd known him well and for a long time. We were actually good friends. Ed had been the general manager of the first team I broke in with in the minors, a club in Scranton, Pennsylvania. The next year he went to Louisville and so did I, and we were there together for two years. My wife and I were close enough to Ed and his family that we named our first child, Eileen, after his wife.

So it was obviously difficult. I had my interests at heart, and he had to protect those of the ball club he worked for. In a situation like that I could never be as hard-nosed as I should have been. A person should never negotiate a business deal with a guy who is a dear friend.

I felt I was in a good bargaining position, however. The Senators had traded six expansion players for me, including Dick Donovan, a first-rate pitcher who, incidentally, would win 20 games for Cleveland that year. And Washington had a dreadful team then. The year before, the Senators had lost 100 games and ended up 10th in the 10-team American League. Mickey Vernon, whom I'd played with at Boston in 1956 and '57, was the manager, and you had to feel sorry for him because he was a fine baseball man. The team just stunk. The only name on its roster that anyone might recognize today was Gene Woodling, and he was 39 years old that year.

I told Doherty, "I'm your man. I'm not your savior, but I'm going to put people in your ballpark. That's got to be worth something." He still said no to the $50,000. Then I remembered something. I said, "How about this? Give me X number of dollars plus five cents a ticket."

I had heard Frank Lane talk about deals like that all the time for guys who could truly bring fans into a ballpark. In fact, I'd almost gotten one like that from him. Doherty wouldn't have any of that, though. I held out until March 8th, but then I went down to Florida, and finally I decided I'd better sign. I did, for $42,500 a year for two years, and then joined spring training. But it was a verbal contract. I am the biggest stupe when it comes to trusting people and shaking hands instead of getting everything written down. Every time I've made a business deal with just a handshake, it hasn't worked. And this would prove to be a perfect example of that.

Playing in Washington was totally depressing. The team was so piss-poor that we'd cinched last place by the first of

A pair of baseball youngsters, holding the cake: Piersall and Billy Martin. Both came to the big leagues in 1950.

With his father and foremost fan at Fenway Park in Boston.

Playing the position he hated, shortstop, in 1952, Piersall tries to complete a double play here. Sliding in is Washington Senator infielder Floyd Baker.

An action shot from the Boston Red Sox days. Piersall is grimacing because the ball has just bounced off him. The Washington catcher is Bob Oldis, and No. 21 is Senator pitcher Maury McDermott. Ducking away from the ball is Piersall's outfield-mate, Jackie Jensen.

With "Dragnet's" Jack Webb.

With the Ted Williams trophy. "One of the greatest honors I ever received," said Piersall.

Piersall steals home during a 1954 Red Sox game. With the bases loaded in the sixth, the run proved to be the game-decider against

the Detroit Tigers. The catcher is Frank House, taking a throw from
Ray Herbert. Looking on is Red Sox outfielder Jackie Jensen.

Sliding in under the fabled Yogi Berra in 1955.

An off-season job, Piersall referees wrestling matches in Cleveland.

With friend, the great slugging shortstop of the Red Sox, Vern Stephens.

A collision with Billy Martin results in some broken ribs. Martin (1) and Detroit second baseman Frank Bolling offer some comfort.

The Most Valuable Red Sox Player award, 1957.

Chatting with umpire Ed Runge at Yankee Stadium in 1958. The other member of the Red Sox is third base coach Del Baker.

Piersall is thrown out of the game at Comiskey Park in 1960 by umpire Cal Drummond. He came back for the second game of the doubleheader and mortified White Sox owner Bill Veeck when he threw a baseball at Veeck's brand-new exploding scoreboard.

Piersall reacts to fans who harassed him on the field at Yankee Stadium in 1961. Kicking a little ass.

Fans on the field in Cleveland. They just wanted to shake hands. Piersall wants no part of it.

After a fight on the field in Cleveland. Piersall charged Detroit pitcher Jim Bunning, then ended up on the bottom of the pile after both dugouts emptied and converged on the pitcher's mound. Looking after him are Indians manager Jimmy Dykes (35) and first baseman Vic Power.

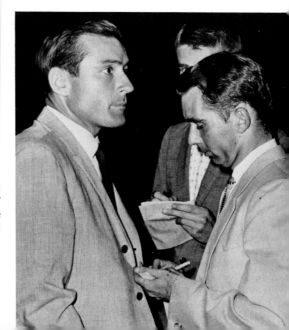

After being thrown out of a game in Cleveland, Piersall is confronted by reporters who want to know if the Indians' management has ordered him to see a psychiatrist.

With an old friend from Massachusetts, President John F. Kennedy, on opening day 1962, when both were Washington, DC, residents.

April. The Senators also opened up their new ballpark that year, and it was a disaster. The field was under water half the time because the drainage system was so bad. It was built on a swamp, and there was no way the water could settle. We wound up wearing football cleats in the outfield there. I can easily say that year with the Senators was my worst in baseball—up to that time.

It started out excitingly enough, however. In fact, opening day in Washington was one of the great thrills of my life. President John F. Kennedy was there to throw out the first ball. There were 50,000 people there, and before the game he sent one of his secret service men to get me and bring me to his box. I'd met him before up in Boston when he was a senator and a Red Sox fan at the time I was playing for them. When I got to his box we shook hands, they took a bunch of pictures of us together, he asked me how my wife and family were, and then he said he wanted to wish me the best of luck as a Washington Senator. I really felt honored. But I also felt like saying to him, "I just don't feel all that happy here, sir," because I knew it was going to be a bum year. And, unfortunately, I was right.

I hurt my ankle in the second series we played that year in Washington. Baltimore was in town, and Brooks Robinson hit a ball into left-center field. I ran back to catch it, but as I went to grab it, my foot went under the fence— they had those chicken wire fences with the crisscrossed spikes at the bottom—and I tore the hell out of my ankle. I still have a helluva scar from it. I didn't play for about three weeks as a result.

When I did come back I didn't do very well. I just finished the season, and it was a real struggle. I had a lot of injuries that year. My shoulder was bothering me. I hurt my wrist in another game, which bothers me to this day. I've been told that one of these days I'll have to have the calcium on it removed surgically. I could hardly swing the bat some of the time.

THE TRUTH HURTS

It was a year of saying: "What am I doing here? Why does this happen to me?" Baseball had been great for me the year before. Now I was making the best money of my life. I had what I thought was the best contract of my life. I wanted to do good. I wanted to help Washington and Mickey Vernon. But I kept getting hurt. And, as it turned out, I was not the guy who was going to lead this team anywhere.

There wasn't anything memorable that year, at least nothing good in terms of baseball. In fact, I wouldn't mind forgetting that season altogether. We ended up with a record of 60 and 101, dead last. I hit only .244.

To give a good idea of the kind of crummy year it was, this was the highlight, the thing I remember most: It happened in September, about the last series of the year. We were playing the Baltimore Orioles. We went over there—we used to take these buses back and forth between Washington and Baltimore. First of all, the bus broke down and we got there late. The buses that the Senators used that year were never checked. I think, because we were such a bad team, the front office was hoping they would break down and we wouldn't have to show up. Some of us were hoping that, too.

Anyway, we got to Baltimore, and I was on the field warming up just before the start of the game. There weren't many fans in the park. But there was one guy with a loud voice, one that you could hear from one end of the field to the other. And he yelled, "Hey, Piersall, you're nuts. You're a gooney bird."

I yelled back, "Hey, wait a minute, we're all doing awful. What're you getting on me for? The season's over. Why yell at me?"

"You're a nut, and so is your mother!" he shouted.

When I heard that, like a bullet, I went up into the stands after him. I got hold of him, but I couldn't get him the way I wanted to. I tore his shirt a little in the scuffle, and then the ushers pulled me off him. There were more ushers in the ballpark that day than there were fans.

Well, I went back down into the clubhouse before the game. A few minutes later, some police officers came in, about four or five of them. They had been involved in breaking it up, too, and actually had ripped this guy's shirt more than I had. They ripped it off, as a matter of fact. They told me that the guy told them I'd assaulted him and torn his shirt. He wanted to press charges against me—not against the police officers, mind you, who had done the most ripping. I'd have to go down to the police station with them, they told me.

So I got dressed, and they put us both in the paddy wagon. I got in there, and by this time I was really hot. There were cops in between us for obvious reasons.

We got to the police station, and the bail was set at $50 for each of us. I came up with it, but he had only $47. So, he turned to me and said, "Would you lend me three dollars?"

I said, "I'd punch you in the mouth. What do you mean loan you three dollars!"

We had to appear in court on another day. Well, I went with the lawyer from the Washington Senators, and all the ushers involved showed up as witnesses. They didn't like this guy because he used to holler at everybody, insult everybody, and they thought he was just a real asshole.

The judge listened to the case and then called the guy up before the bench and gave him a long spiel about how I had encountered a lot of things in my life and how I didn't need to be bothered by a guy like him. Just because he had paid $3.50 to get into the park, he wasn't entitled to get personal with me or any other ball player, he told him. And, as it turned out, it was the guy who ended up convicted and fined. Later I found out that that judge used to sit in the center field bleachers at Fenway Park while he was going to school at Harvard and used to watch me play for the Red Sox. But I really didn't get a break from him, because the guy was in the wrong and the judge simply knew it. The judge made it clear that fans had no right to call anybody's mother a nut, or call anybody a name, or get personal with a ball player.

The only truly bright spot for me during that otherwise dismal year in Washington was getting to know John F. Kennedy. I got to visit with him several times after that opening day when he had me brought to his box. You see, when President Kennedy got elected, there were a lot of people from the Boston area who were brought down to Washington to work at the White House—security guards, office people, that type. One of them was Mrs. Abe Lincoln, his secretary, whom I knew pretty well. Her husband's name really was Abe! A lot of them, like the president, had been Red Sox fans when I'd played there.

Knowing these people in Washington, I got to go to the White House a number of times that year. I was able to walk around there, talk to different people there. I kept pinching myself. Here, a poor kid from Waterbury, Connecticut, was standing there looking out from the Oval Office, talking with the president of the United States. It was really something. Then, I thought, hell, I paid for part of this place; I guess I've got a right to be here.

One of those times is expecially memorable because it involved my daughter Kathy, who was five years old then. At the time, we had a summer home in Hyannis Port, only about a block from the Kennedy compound. One day in July of 1962 I was on the road with the Senators and my family was up there on the cape. Kathy was playing out in front when the president and his daughter Caroline drove by very slowly. Little Kathy recognized him and yelled, "Hi, Mr. Kennedy!"

Well, the president apparently got a kick out of it because he stopped and said, "Hi, who are you?"

She told him, "I'm Kathy Piersall, and my father is the great baseball player."

The president laughed and said to her, "I know him. I've seen him play. Is your mother home?" She was, and President Kennedy went around and visited with her on the porch for about 10 minutes.

When I heard about it and knew how excited Kathy was about it, I called Mrs. Lincoln at the White House and said, "Would you please thank the president for being so nice to my family?"

She said, "Why don't you tell him yourself? He's right here." He got on the phone, and I thanked him. Then I asked for a favor. I had copies of a photo taken of me with him in his box at the ballpark that opening day, and I asked if he might autograph one for Kathy. He said, "Bring it over, and I'll take care of it." Just like that. Come on over to the White House. Well, I did, and he signed it for Kathy.

I remember another occasion that year when I was there. President Kennedy came down the stairs, and he was really hot. He'd just found out that Congress hadn't passed his medical aid bill or something like that. "Somebody double-crossed me," he said, although I can say his language was a little stronger than that; hell, a lot stronger. It made him very human in my eyes. Then he came over, asked how my family was, and we talked baseball for a little while. That was the last time I saw him before he was assassinated.

I remember that awful day very well. I was playing golf at the Hyannis Port Country Club, with a doctor, an undertaker, and another guy, coincidentally. We were on the 14th hole, I recall just as if it were yesterday, and all of a sudden we saw this secret service car come speeding up. We knew the secret service man, had known him from the neighborhood there, and when he saw us he stopped. He told us that the president had been shot in the head down in Dallas. He asked if Rose Kennedy, the president's mother, was on the course. She used to play just the 16th and 17th holes. She'd be driven up, play her two holes, and then go back to the compound. It was amazing for someone her age. We had heard that she was on the course, playing those holes ahead of us, and we told him that, and he sped off. We were all stunned. Both the doctor and the undertaker said that, if he was shot in the head, he must be dead. It really shocked me. Not since the deaths of my mother and father had anything hit me so hard.

I started the 1963 season with the Senators but shortly afterward was traded to the New York Mets. I had a two-year contract—at least I thought I had—but it had been verbal, and the new general manager there, George Selkirk, wouldn't honor it. He sent me a letter before the season, telling me how lousy I'd played the year before and that he was cutting my salary by 20 percent.

At the same time, I made a commission of $40,000 from a batting tee that I had sold to J. J. Newberry's department store chain. They bought 250,000 of the suckers. So, I figured I'd just walk in and tell Selkirk, "You can stick your money up your ass." But my lawyer told me to take the pay cut, so I did. I was on the payroll then but not altogether welcome, the way I read it. Shortly after that I was gone.

I was traded for Gil Hodges and became the first player in the history of baseball to be traded for a manager. Hodges, who was 38 or 39 then, had played first base a little for the Mets the year before and had never managed a major league team before, but the Senators obtained him only to manage the ball club.

Anyway, I had always dreamed about having the opportunity of playing for Casey Stengel, who was managing the Mets that year. Boy, I was excited at the prospect, so I got over to join them as quickly as possible. I met up with them in St. Louis, just in time to get into the lineup and face Bob Gibson. He struck me out twice, then I singled up the middle right over his left shoulder. The next time up, I went down. He hit me right in the middle of the back with a pitch. That was my welcome to the National League.

I remember an article Arthur Daley wrote in the *New York Times* shortly after I'd joined the Mets, which carried a piece of advice for me. It included an anecdote about Casey. "In the days of the Brooklyn Dodgers of sainted memory, their quaint manager, C. D. Stengel, was taken aback at the oddball antics of Frenchy Bordagaray. Ol' Case took as much as he could stand and then made an announcement.

" 'If there's gonna be a clown on this ball club,' he said, 'I'm it.' "

Then Daley ended his article, "All [Piersall] has to remember is the little speech that Stengel gave Frenchy Bordagaray. The Ol' Perfesser exhausts the entire Mets' quota of screwballs."

Well, Casey, by this time, was about 75 years old, and he used to fall asleep in the dugout about the fifth inning of every game. You couldn't really blame him, I guess; the Mets were such a boring team. And awful. In fact, they were the only team in baseball worse than the Senators. They'd ended up in the National League cellar the year before with a record of 40 and 120, 60 games out of first. Even the Senators won 60 games that year.

One day, a little while after I'd joined the Mets, we were playing the Dodgers, and Sandy Koufax was pitching. And he was throwing aspirin tablets, really taking it to us. Duke Snider and I were sitting on the bench in the dugout— Casey said around that time that all I could do was bunt (the same Casey who said I was the best right fielder he'd ever seen when I was playing for Boston) and that all Duke was good for was hitting sacrifice flies. Duke had come to the Mets in 1963, too. After 16 years as a star with the Dodgers, they sold him outright for something like $40,000.

THE TRUTH HURTS

Anyway, Casey was down at the other end of the bench. It was after the fifth inning, and the ground crew had come out to drag the infield. Casey was snoring away. Sound asleep. Duke looked at me and said, "Go get him."

"What do you mean?" I said.

He pointed out at the field, at the ground crew.

I knew what he was thinking, so I went down to the end of the bench and back into the runway. The ground crew was almost finished. I hollered, "Hey!" real loud. And Casey jumped up and started giving signs to the ground crew.

In the same game, now in the ninth inning, Casey wanted a pinch hitter. He never remembered anyone's name by this time in his life. It was always, "Hey, you," or "You, boy." So, he looked down the dugout and yelled, "Hey, you."

We looked at Snider and said, "He means you, Duke." Snider had just recently come with us, and he didn't know all of Casey's ways yet. Anyway, Duke went up there to face his old teammate Koufax. We were at the Polo Grounds, and he got hold of one and put it into the seats in left field (he who was only good for hitting sacrifice flies). It was his 400th home run. Imagine that, 400 career home runs. Boy, that was great. So, I bought all the newspapers the next day, and there wasn't anything big about Duke's feat, just a little box about it, not more than a paragraph or two on the fact that Duke Snider had just hit his 400th home run. I went up to him in the locker room and handed him the newspapers.

"Hey, Duke," I said. "What the hell is this? One stinking little box, that's all. Big man, gonna be in the Hall of Fame someday, and this is all the press you get for 400 homers?"

He just looked at me and said, "Hit the road, Bush."

"Hey, I got 99 homers, Duke, and when I get my 100th, I'm going coast to coast. See you later."

Well, later that year we were playing the Phillies on a

64

Sunday afternoon. And I had a premonition. This was going to be the day. So, I told the photographers—not the writers, because if it didn't come true, God knows what they'd have written about me—"Look, keep an eye on me today, something's going to happen."

I hadn't hit a home run all season, but I just had the feeling that this would be the day. Well, I went up to the plate, and Dallas Green was pitching for the Phils. We were at home at the Polo Grounds, and it was 247 feet down each foul line. I was going for the home run. On the first pitch, I hit a long foul down the right field line. I kept saying to myself, "You don't have to hit it that far in this ballpark." On the second pitch I hit another long foul, this one down the left field line. Well, the count went to three and two, and then I just wanted to hit the ball. Green let the next pitch go, and I got jammed and hit it straight down the right field line. It stayed fair, 248 feet, and dropped into the seats.

So, I ran around the bases backward. And I ran fast backward because I'd practiced for this, backpedaling. Anyway, running backward, I rounded first, second, and when I got to third I shook hands with Cookie Lavagetto, our third base coach, and then continued on to home plate. The place was going wild. But when I passed Stengel in the dugout, he didn't even smile.

The next morning, I felt I was really going to get some ink on this. Well, there were about eight newspapers in New York then, and it was big in all of them. In one newspaper there was a whole sequence of pictures of me running around the bases backward—not on a sports page, but on the front page of the paper.

So I bought copies of all of them and brought them out to the stadium later that day. I gave them all to Snider.

"Here, Duke," I said. "I told you I was going coast to coast. And that's for only 100 homers. Duke Snider gets four hundred of 'em, big home run hitter, and he just gets a little box. The front page for me! Oh, and I just want you to know, I'm going to be on the Jack Paar show tonight. With Zsa Zsa Gabor. Coast to coast."

The end of the story was not all that great, I guess. A couple of days later I was released by the Mets. Stengel didn't like my act all that much. Maybe I should have paid more attention to Arthur Daley.

I saw Rosalind Russell, who I knew was originally from Waterbury, Connecticut, too. So I went over and introduced myself to her. She said, "I know who you are. Your father used to paint our house in Waterbury." My dad had been a house painter, and it fascinated me, stunned me in fact, that she remembered my father from all those years ago. She said then, "And you know, Jimmy, every morning when I get up I look in the box scores to see how many hits you got."

5
THE CALIFORNIA YEARS

I liked the way the *Los Angeles Times* handled it when I came to California in 1963. A small headline in the sports section reported: "Baseball's Bad Boy Is Now an Angel." Not true, of course, but at least I was wearing an Angels uniform.

I came to Los Angeles midway through the '63 season, getting the break of my baseball life when the Angels signed me. I really had had nowhere else to go. The Mets had released me outright in July, and I was gone from major league baseball for the first time since I stuck as a rookie in 1952.

It was rather interesting how I hooked up with the Angels in the first place. After the Mets released me, I went across the Harlem River bridge, from the Polo Grounds to Yankee Stadium, and walked into Ralph Houk's office. He was managing the Yankees that year, and I said to him, "Ralph, I really need some advice. How do I go about talking to somebody in a baseball organization about a job? Do I talk to the manager? The general manager?"

"You talk to the one you know best," he said. "Hell, I'd sign you right now, but I need a pitcher." He also had Mickey Mantle in center field.

After I talked with Houk, I went across the hall to the Angels' locker room; they were in town to play the Yankees that day. I talked to Bill Rigney, their manager and a guy I'd known for a long time. The result was that the Angels signed me that very day.

Well, needless to say, I was happy about that. But the next day the Yankees were playing Baltimore and Mickey Mantle broke his foot. And here I had already signed with the Angels. If I hadn't, Houk would have signed me. That is the closest I ever came to playing for the Yankees, and they went on to the World Series that year and won it big.

So, instead, I went out to California. And I must admit that I was nervous about it. All the normal kinds of fears. What was California going to be like? I'd been there before, but I'd never lived out there. I'd heard about the fast life, especially in Los Angeles and Hollywood. I'd heard how it was very expensive to live out there and how people were supposed to be very distant. But when I got to LA, one of the first things that happened was I met this guy by the name of Denny Weinberg. He was a race car driver. We got to talking, and he told me he was in the process of getting divorced. He said he had an apartment and that I was welcome to move in if I wanted. Well, that was a great break because I was out there alone—again, I didn't want to uproot my family, not knowing how long I'd be there or what it was going to be like. In addition, Weinberg knew everybody around Los Angeles. His father was a multimillionaire, but all Denny wanted to do was race cars. Through him I got to meet a lot of people out there, and everything began to work out nicely.

I was relaxed in California, and I started to play ball really well again. The first game I went four for five against Hoyt Wilhelm. Before, I couldn't hit Wilhelm with a broom. But then I got a bad break. After a couple of weeks, I pulled a hamstring, the first time in my career that that had happened. I was out for the rest of the season, but I'd been batting above .300 in the 18 games I played out there.

At the same time, the layoff enabled me to get around a bit. I got to know Hollywood and met a lot of the famous celebrities who hung around that town. I was pinching myself again. Here was this poor kid from Waterbury, Connecticut, among all those famous people.

While I was there and not playing ball, I decided to go to acting school. I was lousy. But it was a great experience because I learned a lot. And I worked hard at it, learning to do monologues, all that stuff. I worked with Michael Cole, who was one of the better actors to come out of that class. He went on to star in "Mod Squad," but he was just a bartender then learning how to act. I enjoyed the school, and it would later prove to be a big help to me. I remember the teacher, who said to me, "Jimmy, if everyone here worked as hard as you do at it, they'd be a lot better for it. And even if you're not as natural an actor, you're going to get more jobs than they do. You're going to play yourself, and that's going to work for you." And he was right.

I ended up getting all sorts of jobs on all kinds of shows out there, and I did it by being myself. Lucille Ball had me on her show, and so did Milton Berle and Don Rickles. I did six different commercials that first year, too.

I used to go around to all the talent agencies. I'd carry baseballs with me because all the agents, I found out, were ardent baseball fans. I'd give them an autographed baseball, and they loved it. They would bend over backward to help me get jobs. And they would get them for me. Out of 12 places I went when I started, I got eight jobs.

I even wound up with my own radio show on KABC in Los Angeles. Leo Durocher had had it before, but I got it

71

when he left LA for Houston. It was a talk show, and I'd never done one before. It was great fun, though. They called it "The Jimmy Piersall Show," but I also had a co-host, Alan Slate, who has gone on to become a truly first-rate broadcaster and entertainer. The show ran from seven to nine o'clock, six nights a week.

One thing I found that I was good at was getting little scoops. I always strived to come up with them, and sometimes I managed to get some big ones. I remember when I got Don Drysdale and Sandy Koufax on at the same time. It was while they were holding out together for big money from the Dodgers. That was in 1966. The year before, the two of them had pitched the Dodgers to a pennant. Koufax had posted a record of 26 and 8 with an ERA of 2.04 and was a unanimous Cy Young award winner; Drysdale was 23 and 12 with a 2.78 ERA. They hung together in trying to get salaries of well over $100,000 a year each from the Dodgers, and that was big bucks back in those days. The Dodgers were not known for shoveling money out to their players, not even to their superstars, and it looked for a while like they would not sign the two. It was the talk of the town in sports out there. While all this was going on, Drysdale and Koufax weren't talking to the press or other media. Nobody could get near them, but I got them for my show. They finally signed and helped the Dodgers to another pennant. And Koufax won the Cy Young Award again.

Being a guest on the network shows was a lot of fun. There was one that I especially got a kick out of. One day I got a call from Gary Morton, who was Lucille Ball's second husband. He asked if I would like to be on her show. They wanted to have a baseball player in one particular episode that they were planning. They'd tried Dean Chance, who was a Cy Young Award winner, but he didn't work out for them at the studio. I said I'd love to give it a try. They created a story for the show called "Meet Jimmy

Piersall at Marineland." It was actually shot down there at Marineland. In the show, Lucy's son was supposed to be away at military school, and Lucy was bringing him and a bunch of other kids down to meet me at Marineland and get autographs. In the scene, she came running up to me. "Mr. Piersall, Mr. Piersall," Lucy said.

"What's the matter, Lucy?" I said.

"My son pitched a no-hitter, *a no-hitter!*"

"Gee, that's great," I said. "How'd he do it?"

"He walked everybody."

That show played on and on in reruns for almost 20 years. I think a lot of kids know me more for that particular show than for anything else because it was replayed so often on morning TV. It was a great break for me because I got a lot of speaking engagements and other guest shots as a result.

Another time out there that I'll never forget was when I was playing in one of those ball player/celebrity golf tournaments. I was Kirk Douglas's partner. While we were playing, I think it was on the 16th tee, all of a sudden a ball came rolling up from the fairway and went right through Kirk Douglas's legs. Coming down the fairway after it was Sandy Koufax. When he got near us, I said, "Sandy, I'd like you to meet Kirk Douglas."

Douglas said to him, "You know, Sandy, I've got your baseball card at home."

And Sandy said, "Yeah, sure, Kirk, and I've got your sword in my cellar."

A little while after that golf tournament, I got a call from Kirk Douglas's agent. They were going to honor Kirk at the B'nai B'rith in Beverly Hills, and he wanted me to emcee it. Well, I thought it was wonderful of him. I said I'd love to do it, but I honestly felt I'd be out of my element there. He said okay, he'd tell Kirk my feelings. A little while later, he called me back and said that Kirk really wanted me there, at least on the dais. So, of course, I went. But I was worried about what I was going to say, who was going to be there, that sort of thing. I rented a tuxedo. I'd never rented one before in my life, but I got it, got all sharped up, and went to Beverly Hills. Out front, all you could see were people getting out of Rolls Royces and Mercedes. Except for me— I drove up in a little two-door Ford.

Anyway, we had to go into this big reception room and wait at first, and this gave me a chance to talk to some of the people who were there. The first person I saw that I immediately recognized was Edward G. Robinson. I had always admired him, so I said to myself that I had to go over and introduce myself. And I did. I said, "Mr. Robinson, I just want to thank you for all the wonderful entertainment you gave my father and me over the years. When I was a kid he used to take me to all your movies. We didn't have too much money then, but when we saw your movies my father always said it was money well spent."

He looked at me and said, "Well, that's very nice of you to say. But you know, Jimmy, I'm a big fan of yours, too. I've listened to your talk show many times on my way home from the club or from playing gin. And I want to tell you one thing, and don't forget it: *Never* change your ways."

Well, I haven't forgotten it, and I never did change my ways. But maybe I should have because I've been in constant trouble ever since. Maybe it was the worst piece of advice I ever got in my life, but still, Edward G. Robinson was a great man.

After I talked with him, I saw Rosalind Russell, who I knew was originally from Waterbury, Connecticut, too. So I went over and introduced myself to her. She said, "I know who you are. Your father used to paint our house in Waterbury." My dad had been a house painter, and it fascinated me, stunned me in fact, that she remembered my father from all those years ago. She said then, "And you know, Jimmy, every morning when I get up I look in the box scores to see how many hits you got." That really made me feel good.

When I went on Milton Berle's show, it was with Willie Mays and Maury Wills. We had a song that we had rehearsed and were supposed to do with Berle on the show. We had it down, but, as it turned out, Berle couldn't read the song on the cue cards for some reason; at least he couldn't get it right. He was really getting mad about it. Finally, they put the words on a blackboard for him to read, but it still didn't go right, and he got even more furious and cut the song out of the show.

We were still to be on the show, however. We were to appear in our baseball uniforms. Well, we were there for the dress rehearsal before a live audience. We were standing in the wings, and, I guess, because our song was cut out, Willie Mays said to me, "Let's do something to shake him up." He was out there giving the audience his monologue, and I raced out onto the stage and laid down a perfect slide right between his legs. He always stood with them apart, and I went sailing right through and on out into the audience. They went wild, thought it was very funny and part of the show. Miltie was scared shitless by it, though. That was the last time I was on his show.

Fred Haney was the general manager when I joined the Los Angeles Angels. He was a super human being and was always tremendously honest with me in all our dealings. And Bill Rigney, our manager, was also first-class. The team wasn't all that good when I got there, and I wasn't much help because of the hamstring injury I got. In fact, they released me after the season because they didn't know whether I'd be able to make it back.

On the other hand, they did invite me to spring training in 1964, and I went. I was determined to prove that my career wasn't over, although I was 34 years old by then. As it turned out, I did not have a very good spring training. Still, Rigney stood by me and gave me a lot of support. I was signed on then for the '64 season.

It worked out well for all of us. I had a real good year. I played in 72 games and batted .314. Only Tony Oliva of the Minnesota Twins (.323) and Brooks Robinson of the Baltimore Orioles (.317) hit higher than me in the American League that year. Our team did a lot better, too, a record of 82 and 80 and fifth place, which was a helluva lot better than the 70 and 91, ninth place record of a year earlier. Dean Chance won 20 games for us in '64 with a 1.65 ERA and 11 shutouts. When the season was over, the Associated Press named me Comeback Player of the Year, just nosing out Moose Skowron, who had had a fine year with the Washington Senators. At the time, I was quoted as saying it was "my biggest thrill in baseball." Well, it was certainly one of them. I had been worried about whether I could play anymore in spring training, and then everything worked out so well. I mean after Washington and then the Mets and finally getting hurt in LA and realizing at the same time I was moving into my mid-30s, there was reason to worry. A lot of the credit must go to Bill Rigney and Fred Haney, though. Both of them stood behind me, encouraged me, and then gave me the opportunity to make the comeback. After the season, Fred Haney told me I had a job with the Angels as long as he was there. Things were going so well that I brought my family out, and we rented a nice house out in the San Fernando Valley.

With ball playing, the radio show, television guest spots, and public appearances, I really got around in LA during the four years I was there. I had more calls on the banquet circuit during that time than I could handle. I put together all my own speeches. I used to introduce myself as "the greatest diaper changer in the history of baseball" because by that time I had nine kids and it seemed everybody in the world knew that fact. I'd also tell my audiences that I was the only player in baseball who could claim he spent the morning of one day at the White House, the afternoon in jail, and the evening in a hospital. It was true. I had been at the White House, then I got into that altercation with the fan in Baltimore later that day and ended up bailing myself out, and I did walk into a glass revolving door that night and had to get a couple of stitches as a result.

I also liked to tell stories about other ball players. One I especially liked was about Yogi Berra. His kids were moving along in school then, and sometimes they would come home and ask him questions about history and geography. He said he couldn't help them, didn't know much about those subjects. Well, somebody from the audience shouted, "Why don't you buy them an encyclopedia?" Yogi blinked a couple of times and then said back to the guy, "I walked to school; so can they!"

But, as it would turn out, 1964 was my last really good year in baseball. In 1965, I played in only 41 games, but I managed to hit .268. As a team, we finished in seventh place.

I did, however, contribute something in another way that year. Bill Rigney asked me to work as an outfield coach as well as play. I did not want to feel that I was not contributing my share to the team for the salary I was getting, and Rigney knew that. I worked closely with Willie Smith, Albie Pearson, and Jose Cardenal. Jose was only 21 and had just come with us in 1965. He had a great deal of promise, I could tell, but he was trying to act like Willie Mays, do things that maybe Mays could do and get away with but things that nobody else should try. Jose would carry his bat along with him as he was running to first base, for example. Or he would flip the ball back to the infield instead of throwing it hard, and by doing that he often gave the base runner a chance for an extra base. Jose had a natural tendency toward the flair.

Jose didn't realize it, however, but he was making himself look bad, me look bad, and Rigney look bad. And I couldn't get him to stop. Sooner or later, it was going to hurt him badly, I felt.

I remember one day when Jose really got to me. We were playing a doubleheader with Washington, and in the first game he fielded a ball and then just flipped it back into the infield. Well, the guy who hit it to him stretched it all the way into a triple, and that ended up costing us the game. I really was hot about it and got all over him in the dugout. Rigney was mad as hell, too. I went to Rigney and said, "Hell, put me in the outfield next game instead of him, will you?" He did, and I had a super game. I got a triple, hit it over the head of Don Lock, their center fielder; made a diving catch; threw the ball hard and well on some other plays.

After the game, Jose came up to me with a big smile on his face and said, "I see, old man, what you saying." But he still didn't change his ways.

Then I got an idea. I went to his wife, who was nice and a really strong lady. I said to her, "Hey, do you want to make a lot of money? Have a nice house? Fancy cars?"

She said, "Sure."

"Well, you can," I said, "if Jose makes it like I know he can in the big leagues. But he won't unless we can get him to get rid of his bad habits. Maybe you can do it. Get him to stop carrying the bat down to first base. Get him to throw the ball back to the infield right and not just flip it. Get him to hustle all the time, even when things are going badly. He's got to use the tools he's got to make him a good ball player. Otherwise you're never going to get the money or all the other things."

She understood. And obviously she got to him. Almost overnight Jose turned it all around. We had tried and gotten nowhere. It was his wife, strong gal that she was, who got him to do it. And he became a pretty darn good ball player, one who stayed in the major leagues for 18 years.

That was also the year I broke my kneecap. I'd started out pretty well and was hitting okay. Then it happened. It was in a game we were playing against the Minnesota Twins. I was in left field that day, and Zoilo Versalles, their shortstop, hit a long fly ball down the left field line. That year the Angels were playing their home games at Dodgers Stadium, and there was a cinder track there that ran around the playing field. I slipped on it as I was catching the ball and whacked my knee into the foul pole. It really hurt, and I lay there for a bit. The trainer came out and looked at it and said, "C'mon, Hollywood, get up. You're okay. This isn't act three, scene four."

I got up and stayed in the game even though my knee hurt like hell, but it was the ninth inning and I figured I could handle it. As a matter of fact, I caught the last out, a fly ball that was hit right at me. If I'd had to move for it, I'm sure I wouldn't have gotten it.

The next morning, however, I couldn't get out of bed. They sent me to a doctor in order to get the knee x-rayed, and he told me that the kneecap was broken. He also said that I would probably not be able to play ball again. I was supposed to be in a cast for seven weeks. Well, I was out of it in five weeks, but then I broke the adhesions shortly afterward when I was out riding a bicycle up a hill with a couple of my kids.

Still, I made it back into uniform later that year. But I wasn't able to do a lot. I do remember one game in particular after I came back, a kind of last moment of glory, I guess. And it was funny how it happened.

We were playing the Twins again, and Jim Kaat was pitching for them. We had runners on first and second with one out. I got the bunt sign from Rigney, but after the first pitch was a ball, he took it off. So, on the next pitch, I faked the bunt and everybody came rushing in. Then I pulled back and hit the ball. I was off balance when I hit it, but I got good wood on it. I didn't see where the hell the ball went, just took off for first. When I finally saw it, I could see it was line drive, and it just seemed to keep going and going. It ended up in the left-center field seats, and there was no one in the ballpark more surprised than me. Or happier. That was my last major league home run.

The next year, 1966, I played in 63 games but was used mostly as a pinch hitter. I batted only .211, and I knew age was finally catching up with me. I was 36 that year. But I lasted the season.

In 1967, I realized for certain that I couldn't play anymore. I went to bat three times against Detroit, and Mickey Lolich struck me out each time, a pitcher whom I'd hit pretty well against in the past. I went in after the game and told Bill Rigney I was through. I just couldn't do it anymore. At 37 years, it was all over for me.

I had made it through 17 baseball seasons in the major leagues. And no one can say that they didn't know I was around during those years. That's a long career in baseball, and I loved it with all my heart. Now I had to figure out what life would be like without baseball. And that was not going to be an easy thing to do.

I used to get on the referees, too. After all, they're no different from umpires; they just wear different shirts. We used to pay them at halftime of our games. If I was really hot at them, I'd just walk in, drop the money on the floor, and walk out. Sometimes I'd really go whacko. . . . One game up in Long Island there was an obvious interference with one of our pass receivers. Everybody in the place saw it. But the referee, a real homer, was standing there and didn't call it. . . . I called him every name I could think of from the sidelines. I got 60 yards in penalties on that one.

6
LIFE AFTER BASEBALL

Being out of baseball, I guess you could say I was somewhat lost, certainly out of my element. After retiring, I went, in a couple of years, from being the general manager of a minor league football team in Roanoke to, of all things, running a hotel whose one claim to fame was that it had once been the biggest whorehouse in Virginia.

And I got divorced. That was in the winter of 1968, and I was still in California, although I was no longer with the Angels. Fred Haney, who had guaranteed me a job with the ball club as long as he was there, had lost his job, so I was gone, too. Anyway, by this time things weren't working out between my wife and me, so we agreed to end it. I went to Juarez, Mexico, and got it done and that was it. I think it cost $200.

Now I had to start all parts of my life over. First I had to find a job. I began looking everywhere, contacting every-one I knew. One friend of mine in Washington, DC, Greenie Fischer, called me up one day and said he might have a job for me back east. "How would you like to be the general manager of a football team?" he asked.

"What do you mean," I said. "I don't have the remotest idea what a football general manager does."

"All you have to do is sell tickets, do some public relations work, maybe a little television promotion. You just have to look after the operations. You can handle it."

The idea came up at a poker game that Fischer was playing. A guy by the name of Kaufman, who owned Kay jewelry stores, a big chain, owned a team back in Roanoke, Virginia. He said he needed somebody to run it, and Greenie said, "How about Jimmy Piersall? He's looking for a job. Kaufman went along with it.

Well, I had no other job offers. And he was offering me something like $17,000 a year. At the same time, I was a little reluctant to leave California. I'd gotten to like it out there, and at the time I was living with this super gal who was a dancer on the "Dean Martin Show." But as hard as I looked for something around LA, I couldn't come up with anything. So I packed up and moved back east.

The football team was the Virginia Sailors, and they played in the Atlantic Coast Football League, which was quite a popular thing at the time. They had teams in all kinds of cities where there weren't any NFL franchises— places like Hartford, Connecticut; Long Island, New York; Orlando, Florida. They played damn good football, too. In the league, we had quite a few players who later would play in the NFL, like Manny Sistrunk, who would play for the Washington Redskins; Marv Hubbard, who went with the Oakland Raiders; Ted Vactor, another Redskin.

The Virginia Sailors were not a bad team, and they had been developing some good ball players there. And it was not a small-time operation; in fact, it was really a pro league rather than semipro. Their payroll was $5,000 a week. I didn't have any idea how in hell I was going to handle running it. I was scared to death, as a matter of fact. I didn't know a living soul in Roanoke, either.

I figured I had to make it work. It was all I had, and I didn't want to blow it. Besides, I'm a company man, and if I'm hired to do a job, I work my ass off at it. Well, I got there, moved into an office, met the people, and started to get the thing going the best way I knew how.

I worked out a deal with this very fancy hotel there, the Hotel Roanoke. They gave me a nice room for $100 a month, maid service and everything. The manager was a big sports nut, and I'd give him free tickets to our games, get the players to come over, things like that.

One of the first things I did was to change the team's name. We had an arrangement with the Washington Redskins; we would use players from their taxi squad as regulars on our team. They would send players down to us just like in baseball when a major league team would send a player down to the minors. Well, because of our association I got the idea of Buckskins. I held a contest there in Roanoke to give the team a new name, a kind of promotion to arouse interest in the team. But I rigged it so that the name came out Roanoke Buckskins.

Another thing I saw that they truly needed was to get more people into the ballpark—we played in a nice one called Victory Stadium. So I really went after selling season tickets, and I got 5,000 of them sold myself. I had people working the telephones, doing all kinds of promotions to get tickets sold.

We had a special promotion for the opening exhibition game to build interest and hopefully a following for the team. There had just been a bad flood in Virginia, and, along with some of the civic groups, we worked to get relief for the flood victims. We said we'd let anybody into the game free who brought a can of food to the ballpark. We drew more than 13,000 people to it, and there were stacks of canned foods everywhere. We filled six trucks with them.

THE TRUTH HURTS

The Washington Redskins were a big help, too. I went to their offices and talked with their people. They gave me sample brochures and flyers and advice on how to go about selling tickets.

By the start of the season we were drawing about 12,000 to a home game. But if it rained, we were in real trouble. People did not come out in the rain to watch an Atlantic Coast Football League game like they would an NFL game. We were doing a lot better than they had the year before, though, when they lost something like $200,000.

Our season on the field was not too bad. But we lost our first three games. So I went into the clubhouse—or locker room, I guess you call it in football—and harangued the players after the game. I shouted at them, "Hey, it took me five months to get these people to pay to watch you guys play, and in three games of football you're driving them out of the park. They came to watch you guys play, so give them a good ball game to watch, for chrissake."

The coach never liked it when I'd get on his players. And he told me so. I'd say to him, "Hey, pal, you can go, too!" But he was pretty good, and I really didn't bother him much except for yelling at his players. He knew more about coaching football than I did, and I respected that. I just wanted them to go out and win ball games because that's what they were there for and that's what the people came to see.

I had a couple of run-ins with the police down there in the beginning. Under our contract with the city, they provided 16 cops for each game. At the first one, I was walking around and ended up in the ticket office where they were counting up all the money. But there was no cop around. Some were out talking to girls in the stands; some were hanging around the refreshment stands drinking free coffee. I went to the one in charge, whose name was Dick Tracy, no lie, and said, "Hey, you know somebody could come in and steal this money. You think we could bother one of your men to provide us a little protection?"

"Don't bother me," he said.

Well, I told him what I thought, and he couldn't believe it. From that time I was in a lot of hot water with the Roanoke police, especially Dick Tracy. But I didn't care. I kept going around during the games and got on them if they were just loafing around. Once Tracy threatened to throw me in the clink for using "abusive language to a police officer."

I used to get on the referees, too. After all, they're no different from umpires; they just wear different shirts. We used to pay them at halftime of the games. If I was really hot at them, I'd just walk in, drop the money on the floor, and walk out. Sometimes I'd really go whacko. I didn't want to yell at our players, so if things weren't going right, I'd yell like hell at the referees. I'd come down to the sidelines and get all over their asses. One game up in Long Island there was an obvious interference with one of our pass receivers. Everybody in the place saw it. But the referee, a real homer, was standing right there and didn't call it. I went bananas. I called him every name I could think of from the sidelines. I got 60 yards in penalties on that one. Everytime I said something he walked off another 15 yards.

We had a pretty good year on the field, as it turned out, and it was the best year they'd had financially. We lost only about $20,000, a 10th of what they had lost the year before. At the end of the season, Mr. Kaufman said he was going to give me a two-year contract at $25,000 per. I was delighted. With that in my pocket, or at least thinking that it was, I decided to get married again. The girl was Marigay Hamlett, who worked for the Chamber of Commerce in Roanoke.

Well, once again I didn't have a written contract, just a handshake. And not too long after I got married, Mr. Kaufman called me up and told me I'd better start looking for a different job. He was getting out of the minor league football business.

So, of all people, my brother-in-law, Richard Hamlett, bought the team from him. I'd told him he was nuts to buy it, that he was going to lose too much money on it. But he went ahead and bought it anyway and hired me to run it for him. He was a very successful contractor and had his hands in a lot of business ventures. Not too long ago he married Debbie Reynolds. It was a hobby to him, the football team. He loved the football players, hero-worshipped them. If they wanted something, he'd give it to them or get it for them. If they wanted to borrow money, he'd go right into his pocket for it. I told him not to give them anything except their salaries. Anyway, we got into a big argument about who was running the team and how it was being run, and he fired me. He decided to run it himself.

I thought I might be able to get a job with Whitey Herzog, maybe managing or coaching with the minor league team in Richmond. But I didn't go over there.

My brother-in-law also had me running this hotel, the Crystal Tower, for him. He'd just bought it, and it had at one time been the biggest whorehouse in Virginia. It was said that the bell captain there had been making $70,000 a year, not bad in those days.

I remember when he told me he wanted me to manage it. I said, "What the hell do you want me for? I don't know anything about running a hotel." Then I figured, "What the hell?" I didn't have a job, so I went to work running his hotel. And I was tough. I'd get there at 5:30 in the morning. I watched everybody and found out they were all rotten there. I fired all the maids because they were stealing everything they could get their little hands on. And the maintenance people weren't any better, so I fired them, too. The waitresses were eating all his food and drinking his booze and giving it away to their boyfriends. They didn't give a crap about the customers, so I got rid of most of them, too.

He had this rock and roll group playing there, and all it would draw was a bunch of long-haired kids who would buy one beer and sit there all night. I got rid of them and got a group that would bring in some older people who would spend some money.

One thing my brother-in-law didn't like was when I chewed out one of his girlfriends. He had her on the payroll, and she was worthless, didn't do a damn thing. I mean she came to work wearing a mink coat. I got all over her about that.

I worried about his money as if it were my own—more than he did, as a matter of fact. But after a while he fired me from that job, too. I didn't really care all that much; the hotel business was not for me. I wanted to get back into baseball in one form or another. And I got my chance in 1972. What I had no way of knowing, however, was that it would be one of the most chaotic, frustrating, maddening, and depressing years of my life.

Finley ran from bus to bus, shouting like a madman. I was outside the airport, over near the airplane, standing by the mule now, who had just been unloaded, and I shook my head and said to it, "Listen to that son of a bitch; he's goofier than both of us."

7
THE FINLEY FIASCO

Charlie Finley was an awful person. But I didn't know that when I called him about a job in 1972; at least I didn't know it firsthand. I really needed a job then. And I was very pleased that he gave me one in the Oakland front office. I also felt he really needed me because he was having a desperate problem with his ticket sales. With a really good ball club, he wasn't drawing at all. His group ticket sales were only about 50,000 the previous year.

Well, he told me to come to Chicago and meet with him. That's where he ran his business. I packed up everything and drove in from Roanoke. I spent some time with him, and he explained what he wanted me to do. We shook hands, and that was it. We had a deal, he said. He wanted me to handle group ticket sales for the As, and the deal was that I would get 20 percent of what I sold, and I'd get a draw against my commissions.

It sounded good to me, and it would get me back into baseball, so I took it. I left my car in Chicago and flew to Oakland the next day.

THE TRUTH HURTS

When I got out to California the strike was already on, which slowed things down for me—you can't sell tickets when no ball games are being played. Still, it gave me the chance to get to know the area and set up my program: what I was going to do, whom I was going to call on, that sort of thing. I also had time to arrange some speaking dates, to get some recognition out there. I knew that would help later in my group ticket sales efforts, and it really did.

I had been told that Finley was a rotten bastard to work for and that he was probably the most unappreciative son of a bitch in the world. "You'll find out as soon as you work for him for a while," I was told. But I kind of didn't believe it because I was happy with the way he accepted me, and I'd known him for years and had always gotten along with him, although it was just on a conversational basis. In fact, I guess I could say I had respect for him at that point.

When I got out there I didn't see much of him. He was wrapped up with the pro basketball team and the professional hockey team that he also owned. He told me he bought the baseball team, the As, in Kansas City for about $1.2 million, which was unbelievable. And he got the pro basketball team for about $90,000. But he was more excited about getting all the nice office furniture that went with it than he was about the basketball team itself. He got the hockey team for about a million, I'm told, and he sold it for somewhere between three and five million. On the basketball team he made a bundle, too. And the As, well, he sold them for about $14 million. I've got to give him credit, he knew how to work in the black. It was dealing with people that was his problem.

With all he had going on, Finley didn't have a lot of time for me when I was first out there. I didn't realize what a blessing that was. Anyway, I just went out on my own, setting things up, and everything was fine between us.

As a matter of fact, when I got out there he let me use his apartment. He had a big one in downtown Oakland, about four bedrooms in a high-rise. His apartment covered half of the top floor. A free place to live, that was nice. But when I moved in, it was a real surprise. In this elegant apartment building, his apartment was a pigpen. I'd never seen anything like it. I mean there were chicken bones on the floor, garbage all over. It was filthy. It took me two solid days to clean up the place. Everywhere, in the living room, kitchen, bathrooms, bedrooms, it was a sty.

Finley liked to wear the colors of the ball club—green, yellow, and white. He'd wear specially made green or yellow sports jackets, very nice ones. He was always neat, clean, on the outside anyway, but that apartment was a disaster. It was my first inkling that Finley was a little on the strange side.

When the strike ended and they started to play ball again, Finley said he wanted me on the radio, too. One day he just came up to me and said, "You're going to be on in the fifth inning; do the play-by-play." He was getting a lot of money from Arco and Dodge, the sponsors, and he wanted some of it to pay my expenses and some of my commissions. He wanted to get it from there instead of from the organization's pocketbook, which was fine by me. It was another job. But it didn't make things easy. I'd be at the ballpark 'til one in the morning most nights and then up in the morning to do my regular job.

I did say to him, "Hey, I'm not ready to do play-by-play. It wouldn't be fair to the other announcers."

"Don't worry about it," he said. "You do what I tell you to. I'll handle them."

So I did it, and I was terrible. I'm sure I could have done the color on the spur of the moment, but not the play-by-play. The announcers, Monte Moore and Jim Woods, were very patient, but I was bad. As time went on, however, I realized that the exposure could help in my group ticket sales efforts.

The As, as I mentioned earlier, weren't drawing well

then. I'd call on big accounts in Oakland, San Francisco, Sacramento, San Jose—really big ones like IBM and Lockheed, each with about 15,000 employees. But they weren't very receptive to me because Finley had handled this before and had already alienated them. They were very unhappy with him. His attitude had been that he was doing them a favor by talking to them and letting them come to his ballpark.

Besides being sore at Finley, the companies had other alternatives. We had to go head to head with the San Francisco Giants. They were just across the bay and were very aggressive, offering good deals to the companies or groups, discounts on tickets, that sort of thing. I told Finley that we had to do the same thing if we were to compete. He threw his hands up in the air. "The hell we do," he said. "We don't have to give them anything. We're the class out here." Well, I went ahead and did it anyway, gave discounts, because that was the *only* way I could sell any tickets. He would find out about it when I turned in my reports and then get pissed off, but we at least sold some tickets and I earned my commissions.

I'm not kidding when I say it was tough out there. You have to remember that there were so many things to do in California, that people had a lot of choices. The San Francisco/Oakland area was a great recreational area, with so many things for families to do. There were two pro football teams, two professional baseball teams, a pro basketball team, and all the college teams. And Oakland and San Francisco aren't actually all that big. Oakland had only about 350,000 people, and I don't think San Francisco was over 750,000. So I really had a lot of competition, but Finley couldn't understand that. We were lucky if we could draw a million people over a season when he had the ball club. Since he's been gone, they've got attendance figures like 1.9 million.

A good example of how it was in those days is the promotion I set up with the Shriners. Finley himself was a

Shriner. I got the idea to have a Shriners night at the ball-park. So I got the top Shriners together, and we worked things out to have a contest between the Oakland and San Francisco Shriners to see who could produce the best turnout. I gave $1 back to them on each ticket they bought so they could raise money for their hospital out there. They sold 20,000 seats. It was really a terrific promotion.

I asked Finley to present the check, for more than $20,000, to them when it was all over. He gave them the check, beaming. In the spotlight, he was in his glory, and he handed it over smiling away. Then he had a stroke with me for giving them a dollar rebate on the tickets. He raged at me.

One of the basic problems was that it wasn't *his* idea. He didn't like anyone else to get the credit for a good idea. He resented it. I learned from it, and in the future I'd usually go up to him beforehand and ask, "What do you think of this, Charlie? What do you think of that?" Then, when it happened later and he was happy about it, he would think it had been his idea.

During the season Finley would come out from Chicago and spend a few days every once in a while. Sometimes he would cook dinner in the apartment. He loved to cook and was pretty good at it. His favorite was meatloaf, and he made a damn good one. But he also made an awful mess and would just leave it. I'd have to clean it up afterward.

While he was there at the apartment we would often talk about baseball, and he would tell me whom he was going to trade and so on. Then he'd say, "Now don't tell *any-body*." Then, an hour later, we would go to the grocery store. He loved to do that, too. He liked to pick things out. He'd play catch with a cabbage, throw it to this Chinese guy who was working in vegetables. And he'd then get talking to him and tell him all about the trade he was going to make, the same thing he told me *not* to tell anybody about.

When he was in Chicago he would call at 6:30 in the

morning Pacific Coast time, and want me to read the Oakland and San Francisco papers to him. He was dying to hear what they had to say about him. "Is there anything in there about me?" he would ask. Never: "Is there anything about the team?" Just "me." So I would read what there was to him, and then when I finished he would say something like, "You're a lousy reader." And I would say, "Well, what are you calling me for then?" He had an ego, a huge one.

Other times he would call and want me to turn the radio on to the game and hold the telephone next to it so he could listen. I used to tell him, "Hell, you can have that piped directly to you out there, if you want." But he would ignore that and then would ask me questions between innings. "What would you have done there?" he'd ask. I'd say, "I don't know the team that well." I didn't want to answer questions like those. I really didn't know the team that well at that point, and I didn't want to second-guess Dick Williams, the manager. It would make Finley mad, and he would say, "Aw, hell, you're just another jockstrap."

One morning at the apartment, at about five o'clock, he banged on my bedroom door. I came out, still half asleep, and he was storming around, saying one minute, "I'm going to fire Dick Williams," and the next minute, "I need some coffee." Then he shook his head. "What am I going to do with this pitching staff?" he said. "I've got the best relief pitchers in baseball—I went out and got them myself—and still we're losing games." He was referring to Rollie Fingers and Bob Locker and Darold Knowles. What had been happening for about four days was that Williams would go out to the mound to take a pitcher out, and the pitcher would talk him into one more pitch. These were very good pitchers: Catfish Hunter, Vida Blue, Ken Holtzman, Blue Moon Odom. Well, at that time, it turned out that that next pitch was usually hit out of the park or whacked somewhere to score a run. And it did cost us first place when the Texas Rangers beat us in a doubleheader on a Sunday in

July and took over first. It was after that that Finley was raging about in the apartment. He was going to fire Williams and the pitching coach, Bill Posdell. He asked me what I would do if I had the best pitching staff in baseball.

I thought for a little bit—being an old jock, I didn't want to hurt Williams and Posdell—so I came up with this idea: Tell Williams that from now on when he goes to the mound to give a signal to the bullpen at the foul line. Touch his left arm if he wants a lefty, his right arm for a righty. That way the pitcher won't get a chance to talk Williams out of taking him out.

Finley liked the idea. Then he got on the phone—it was six o'clock in the morning—and told him he wanted both Williams and Posdell over there for a meeting. Then he told me to get lost. The next night I saw Williams give the sign at the foul line. He brought in a lefthander, Darrold Knowles, and it worked. Finley was ecstatic. He jumped up in his box and waved at me over in the broadcast booth. The As went on to win, regained first place, and stayed there through the World Series.

He was not just a meddler; Finley *ran* the ball club. I give him credit for getting things the way he wanted them on the team, and it did result in a pennant. But he would call the manager 90 times a day. The poor guy could never sleep. He would have to take the phone off the hook. I used to hide from the telephone on weekends. The manager, me, everybody—he was constantly calling us.

Another thing he did that infuriated everybody was to keep track personally of our mileage and our gas—some of us had company cars. But you couldn't buy gas on the weekends with a credit card. If you did, he could tell, and he'd get mad as hell. "What are you doing using the car on the weekend?" he'd shout. He was sure you were using it for personal reasons. In fact, he didn't really like the idea of your having a day off at all. He would have had an eight-day work week if he could have arranged it. And he was always calling me up to check on someone else—what they were doing, where they were, why they weren't doing something—and then he would call somebody else to check up on me.

Besides the goofy things Finley did, which you learned to live with, there was also the fact that you never knew just what to expect from him. You would think things were going along fine, and suddenly he would explode about something, usually nothing important. I remember once riding in a car with him on the way to a game. I told him I had to speak to a group in the wine belt, the Napa Valley, that night. It was for the ball club, and about 500 people were scheduled to be there. It was a long drive from Oakland, so I told him I thought I would leave after the fifth inning, after I finished my part on the radio. He turned and looked at me like I was crazy and then started screaming. I mean he went bananas. "What do you mean, leave? Who do you think you are? You aren't running this ball club."

I couldn't believe it. Nobody ever shouted at me like that, treated me that way. I said, "Hey, you better not ever holler at me like that again." I was really mad. Here I was, a company man. I was going up to sell tickets for him. But he did that kind of thing to everybody who worked for him.

Sometimes he would call me at the office out at the ball-park, and if I was out selling tickets somewhere, he would get hold of me later and tell me I should spend more time in the office. What the hell was I doing out all the time? But if I was there when he called, he would ask me later why the hell I wasn't out somewhere selling tickets. "That's what I pay you for," he'd say. "Why aren't you out there making sales calls, with a pocketful of dimes so you can answer your messages?"

On the outside, though, he was a charmer. He ordered big in restaurants, picked up the tabs, even though he didn't always have the money in his pocket. He often asked me for the cash to pay the bill, and it was usually hard as hell to get it back. Ordinarily, I'd have to go take it out of petty cash. But to outsiders he was a big spender, liked to be the big shot. He would give a big tip to a waitress, or he would send over an Oakland As jacket or an autographed baseball for her kids.

A lot of times we would eat out after a Sunday game. He would take me down to Fisherman's Wharf for dinner, and he would order. He wanted to handle everything, be the center of attention. One day we were sitting in a restaurant down there, and he was getting ready to order. Outside we could see two pretty girls standing there talking. He said to me suddenly, "If you can get those girls in here to have dinner with us, I'll give you $100.

Well, I've got the balls of a burglar, so up I jumped and out I went. I said to them, "Hi, ladies. I'm a stranger in town, and I'm working for a guy who is really a big spender." I told them a little bit about him, talked for a few minutes. Then I asked if they had had dinner. They said no. I said, "Why don't you come in and my boss will buy your dinner. No strings, nothing, just dinner. And I'll give you $25 each because I've got a bet with him for $100 that I can get you to come in and join us. And you'll enjoy this guy because he'll really put it on for you."

So they said, "Why not?" We went in and, boy, Finley was excited. He really put on the dog for them, telling them about himself, ordering for everybody. After dinner, he said, "Why don't you come back to the apartment with us? Jimmy will give you a ride home later." They said they would. Finley was glowing; he was delighted. Well, we got there and went in. Charlie poured a drink for them, then went into the bedroom and went to sleep for the night. The next day he didn't ask anything about it, didn't say *anything* about it, never brought it up again. I paid them out of my own pocket the $50 I promised them. I tried to get the $100 back from Finley later, but I never got it so I just took

THE TRUTH HURTS

$50 out of petty cash and at least I came out even.

But after a while he tried to make me his flunkie. He wanted to make me feel like I was one. He got his kicks that way. He knew I was a personality, that I was known around Oakland, that I had a following. I'd been doing the radio and many, many speaking engagements. He was aware of all this, so he decided to demote me to flunkie.

One of the first things was the mustache wax affair. Because of Rollie Fingers, who had that elaborate mustache, Finley decided to give away mustache wax at the ballpark. He found a way to get it for nothing, and the plan was to pass it out at the gates before the ball game. He told me he wanted me out there handing it out. Here, I'd been working all week, running sales promotions, doing my radio bit, and he wanted me standing out in front of the ballpark passing out mustache wax. I was so taken aback by it that I said I would do it. But I didn't, and he never knew that I didn't.

Then there was Bat Day. He called me at six in the morning and told me he wanted me to get over to the ballpark and unload the bats that they were going to give away to the kids that day. I didn't do it, of course.

Charlie Finley wanted a whipping boy. He really enjoyed demeaning people. I seemed to be his choice. Later he found out that I didn't unload his truck, and he was unhappy as hell about it and told me so. I said, "I'm not ever lifting any bats out of a truck for you. I bust my balls all week long for you, doing my job, what I was hired for." But he never saw things in those terms.

After that there were the incidents at the playoffs and the World Series. We had a great ball club that year, a truly great one. And I have to give Finley credit for getting people like Matty Alou for the outfield and Dal Maxvill, the shortstop; they helped make the difference in the pennant race.

When we got to the playoffs, Finley said he didn't want me on the radio. Why? Who knows. Then he wanted me

100

back on the radio, to do the interviews. I said okay, whatever he wants.

I was doing the postgame interviews, and the most important one was after the last game of the playoffs. We had just beaten Detroit 2–1 and clinched the pennant. I was supposed to interview Finley himself in the dugout. But that had been a wild game, and the fans came rolling out of the center field stands. They knocked down the fences, virtually tore them down. Finley saw them and ran away. Out of the dugout. Just ran away. He was really a gutless guy. And here I was about to go on the radio, the microphone in my hand, and nobody to interview. I saw Al Kaline, and I yelled to him. He came over, and I told him, "Al, I need a favor." He understood and said, "Sure." I got a super interview with an eventual Hall of Famer and a class guy. As it turned out, it was a real pleasure to talk with a real big leaguer instead of a jerk.

Finley was back in the clubhouse and was obviously pissed at me. That's the way he was. When I finally got back there, the players poured champagne on me, threw me in the showers. It was a typical celebration. But Finley didn't like that at all. He said to me, "These are *my* players, and I don't want you mingling with them anymore." I said to myself, this is crazy. Why is he mad at me? I knew then how bad it all was.

The World Series was chaotic as hell. He had done all those things to get us there, but when it came about he didn't even hire any extra people—off-the-field people. Instead he gave everybody all kinds of extra things to do. He told me that he wanted me to put all these pennants on sticks, about 5,000 of them, for this area around the dugout and behind it, his own little cheering section. I told him to get the kids around there to do it. I was not going to sit down and put his pennants together.

Finley not only didn't hire any extra help, but instead of using the hotel for press conferences and meetings, he had this tent set up under the stands. And he used to keep the mule, our mascot, in there. The smell was unbelievable. The mule would piss and shit all over the place. But that is where the press room was, and that's where the writers would eat. The mule also used to lick Finley's bald head. They were quite a pair.

One job Finley did assign me at the series was to look after his mother and father, who were two super people. Well, there was a problem with a place to stay. Somebody was already in Charlie's apartment there in Oakland. So I told Charlie's son to tell him that so he could tell his folks. Well, the kid didn't tell him, and Charlie's parents went to the apartment, walked in, and found somebody there taking a shower.

The next day Finley was really mad at me. He said, "You hurt my mother and father." I told him I didn't hurt his mother and father, that I'd told his son to tell him or them not to go there. In fact, as it was, I looked after his folks throughout the series in Oakland and in Cincinnati, and his mother later wrote me a beautiful note thanking me for the way I'd treated them. But all Charlie would say to me was that I hurt them; that was the only thing he would let into his mind.

The next thing he came up with was that he wanted me to be his runner—that's really what it was—to bring hot dogs and other refreshments to the commissioner and his party in their box.

I was really fucking mad by this time, really hot. So I did it. I went over to Bowie Kuhn's box and said to him, "Commissioner, how do you like having a guy who played 17 years in the big leagues waiting on you? Don't you think it might be embarrassing if they show me on television handing you a hot dog and serving a whole bunch of sodas to your friends here? That a former ball player is now serving as a vendor?" Well, that ended it right there.

Finley would not let Jim Woods, the Oakland announcer, and me go into the clubhouse or onto the field during the series either. He wouldn't give us any press credentials at all. We had to sit way down the left field line during the ball game. The one good thing that came of it was that it enabled me to see the greatest catch made in a World Series since Al Gionfriddo stole the home run from Joe DiMaggio in 1947. Joe Rudi made a catch out there to save a ball game, and it was a sight to behold. Charlie never gave us a reason why he did that to us. I still can't figure that one out.

Finley would do all those things to try to downgrade you. He would get it into his mind that he wanted you to do something menial, and it didn't matter who you were, what you had been hired for. He wanted to put you in your place—his place, and to him that was subservient.

The entire World Series was a madhouse. And Finley certainly helped make it that way. On the airplane between Cincinnati and Oakland, Finley had the band playing. This was the one that had entertained at the game, and he had them playing on the plane. The noise was incredible. And the mule, our mascot, which went everywhere with us, was below in cargo.

Anyway, while all this was going on, Dick Williams, our manager, came up to me on the plane.

"I hear you've been second-guessing me to Finley."

I don't know if he had had a lot to drink, or what, but it really hurt me that he would say that because I prided myself on *not* having said anything to Finley about what should be done, even though he had asked me hundreds of times. I never said anything about how Williams was managing the team or about his decisions on the field. I had respect for Dick Williams, and to this day he does not know that I helped *save* his job that morning back in the apartment.

The wildest was yet to come, however. After the last game, which we won, and after we were on the airplane flying back to Oakland, Finley said to me, "Look, you'll be in charge of getting the players and their wives up on the platform in the airport." He wanted them up there on this stagelike thing, where he was going to introduce them to the crowd that was coming out to greet us.

Well, it's a very small airport in Oakland, and when we got there the place was jammed, literally overflowing. There was only a little path for us to go through the crowd. And they were wild. The people were shouting and screaming and grabbing at the ball players and at their wives. Some of them were even grabbing the wives' tits.

Finally the police chief said to me regarding the ball players and their wives, "Hey, you better get them all out of here, or we'll have a riot. Take them back the way they came." So we turned around and went back out instead of up to Finley's platform. When he found out that we went back, that we weren't coming to meet him, he went berserk. I mean he went truly insane. He came running down from his platform, down the stairs, and caught up to me outside. He was ranting and screaming. "Who the hell told you to let the players go back? Who did this? Who did this to *me*?" And I said, "I did." I told him the chief of police said it was dangerous and we had better get them out of there before somebody got hurt.

Finley yelled, "I don't give a goddam who said that. This is my team. I'll tell them what to do." Then he ran back out onto the runway to see where they had gone. He finally ran over to a bunch of buses that were parked off to the side. All the time he was screaming for them, for the ball players. "You gutless bastards, where are you?"

Finley ran from bus to bus, shouting like a madman. I was outside the airport, over near the airplane, standing by the mule now, which had just been unloaded, and I shook my head and said to it, "Listen to that son of a bitch; he's goofier than both of us."

After the World Series, I knew I couldn't take much more of Charlie Finley. And I didn't.

The last days with Finley had been terrible. After I had

done so much work out there, he told me he now wanted me to sell time on the scoreboard, commercials, which is utterly ridiculous. He gave me prices and all that, but what he was really showing me was that he didn't want me around anymore.

That was just one thing. At the end I no longer had a car. He told me I could no longer use the apartment or the company credit card. He made it clear he had no appreciation whatsoever for anything I'd done out there. He had just lost all memory of it, put it out of his mind. And that's when I figured I had better get out of there.

When the series was over he called me into Chicago for a meeting with him. So I flew there and showed up at his office at the time I was supposed to be there. And I'll be a son of a bitch if he didn't lie on his couch, with me sitting there, and watch the Notre Dame–Southern Cal football game. I had to sit there for three hours and wait until the game was over.

Finally, he got up off his ass, and we talked business. I'd brought records of all the ticket sales I'd made over the year. I told him that, according to my figures, he owed me $20,000 in commissions over and above my draw. I showed him that I'd brought in more than $350,000 in revenue. When I brought the records out he said, "Where the hell did you get those?" I told him I got them from the office out in Oakland. So he called the ticket manager out there and gave him hell. He told him he shouldn't have given the records to me. The guy said, "Why the hell not? You had him on a draw, so he has a right to them." Finley hung up on him. Then he tried to get the treasurer of the ball club, but he couldn't reach him. Well, he was furious now.

He looked at the records and said, "Hell, the girl in the office could have done this on the telephone. I didn't need you to do this." Then he got out the receipts from the World Series and said, "Look at this bill for the limousines; it's your fault I have to pay this bill."

I said, "Hey, Charlie, I asked you if you wanted to try

limousines, and I got you four of them free for a day. Then you fell in love with them and ordered them for everybody."

Then he picked up the phone and called the limousine companies—one in Oakland and the other in Cincinnati—and tried to get them to take season tickets for next year instead of the money he owed them for the limo rentals, about $5,000. Well, they apparently both told him something like, "Kiss my ass." So now he was even madder and was blaming me for the whole limo deal. By this time I just wanted to knock him out the goddam window, right onto Michigan Avenue.

He kept the records that I'd brought and told me again that one of his girls out there could have sold the tickets. What he was saying was that I didn't deserve the commissions and that I wasn't going to get the $20,000.

He told me the meeting was over. I didn't get the $20,000 in commissions. I didn't press it because I didn't have anything in writing, and I felt if I sued him I might not be able to get another job in baseball.

I went back out to Oakland and wrote Finley a note, thanking him for the opportunity to be involved with a pennant-winning team and for the World Series ring. I appreciated it, I said, even if it didn't have a diamond in it. I was glad to get it anyway, although I'm sure it bothered him to give it, even without the diamond. So I quit.

I went back to Roanoke after the Finley thing broke down completely. At the time I was totally drained of confidence in myself. I had this feeling I was a failure. He tried so hard to give me that feeling—I guess he succeeded.

Around the same time I had been having problems with my wife, too. She was in Roanoke, and she was unhappy about a number of things. Don't get me wrong; she was a super person, and we thought the world of each other. It's just that we were having problems and she had not wanted me to come back to Roanoke just then.

So between my wife and the Finley situation, it really hit me, and I got very depressed, into crying and all that, and I went to see a psychiatrist. Actually my wife took me to one. I really didn't want to do it. The psychiatrist told me I had to get away from it all. He said they had a rehab center in the Roanoke Hospital, on the fifth floor. I can even remember the room number. Well, when he told me this, in my mind I knew they lock you up in those places. I wasn't happy about it, but I signed myself in anyway.

After I was in there, however, I got to realizing that I was *both* physically and mentally tired, exhausted, that I had to get myself physically strong again to cope with my mental problems, to be away from everybody and from all the trials and tribulations I'd been going through outside. Suddenly the rehab center seemed to be the place I could do that.

The one thing I did not like was that I had to talk to the psychiatrist. That was the worst thing. But I did it; I sat there for an hour across from him and made up things to talk to him about. The psychiatrist was a real pain in the ass. I used to look over the table at him and say, "You know, doctor, after looking across at you every day, I've finally decided that you are the ugliest son of a bitch I've ever seen in my life. And I really can't stand talking to you." He never said anything when I said that, probably just wrote down in his little book "attitude hostile" or something like that. I also told him, "You know, I'm here because my wife feels it's best for me and I feel it's best for me, but you are not the one who is getting it done. You are just part of something I have to do for myself, nothing more." When I think about it, when I looked at him, that's what made me well.

I wouldn't take the pills either, or the drugs they wanted to give me. Those things can be habit-forming. You get to depend on them. In the beginning I did take sleeping pills, but after I got stronger I wouldn't even take them. When the nurse gave it to me I'd stick it under my tongue, and when she stepped out of the room I'd flip it, throw it down the toilet.

I was in a single room. Others shared a room. It was just like an ordinary hospital room, only most of the time you couldn't get off the fifth floor. But you could walk around the ward, and I did that all the time. I used to walk miles around the ward. It gave me plenty of time to think. My whole life history—I went through it all as I walked. If I had wanted to write a book then and had had a tape recorder with me, it would have been easy.

I also got to see some other people when I took these walks, got to talk to them, know them. These were people with similar problems, younger people, older people, people whose families didn't want them anymore. One of them was a former school principal, another a plant superintendent. There was a farm manager, people from all walks of life. And they ranged in age from 30 to 70.

Some of them were sent there for shock treatments, which made me sad because I felt the shock treatments were bad. They would give you headaches, awful headaches, migraines, that you would never get over. Those treatments didn't help them, and they brought back some memories of my first hospitalization back in the early 1950s. Not a lot, though. It was actually hard for me to remember much about that first hospitalization. It had been so long ago. And most of it was just a big blank. I guess you remember only the things you have to or want to.

I talked to the nurses a lot, too. I got pretty friendly with them. I like people, and I've kind of got this way where I can get little favors from them. For example, we weren't allowed to go outside. But I talked the nurses into taking us out for walks. I set up the first walks outside that they ever had there for the patients on the fifth floor. I convinced the nurses that nobody would run away. Those walks outside were more therapeutic for the patients than anything the psychiatrists were doing inside the hospital. The walks and our talking together helped to build confidence in all of us.

I stayed at the rehab center for about a month. Charlie Finley called me once while I was there, but I didn't take the call and never called him back. I learned to play bridge there. I learned to do pottery. Anything to keep active. I'd go downstairs to the exercise room; they would let you do that. And I'd do all the exercises. Hours of them. I got myself into good physical shape. What I needed to do was to get back the attitude, "*I* can do it!" I had to get back my self-confidence.

I'd always prided myself on being a fighter, standing up for what I believed. There are, however, weak points in your life, in everybody's life, and you have to go through them. But finally I got back in shape. I felt strong, and the attitude was good again.

Near the end I got a call to manage a minor league ball club in Orangeburg, South Carolina. This was great because now I could tell the doctor that I'd found a place to go, a job to manage a baseball team. As it turned out, I had to go to the doctor and beg, plead, cajole to get myself released. In other words, I had to bullshit him into letting me go. The power to let me go was solely his, and that, as far as I was and am concerned, is very wrong.

The guy who had called, Red Dwyer, didn't know I was in the rehab center; he just thought I was in the hospital for some minor thing.

So the doctor finally released me, and I went down there. Later my wife came down to South Carolina, too, and that helped a lot. And we had fun. I lost all the stuff that had been bothering me. I forgot about the rehab center. And I was over Charlie Finley. Things were looking up considerably.

It was awful. What a scary thing. Here they were going to operate on my heart. I was due to check in at seven o'clock. I got there, but I didn't go in. I just drove around for about four hours. I didn't want to go through with it, but I knew I had to. It's a terrible feeling when you have to face something like that. You just wish that things would change, that it was all just a bad dream, that it wasn't really happening to you. But it was . . . I told the doctor on duty, "I want a shot, bang, knock me out. When I wake up in the morning I want another shot, bang. I don't want to be awake. I don't want to see anybody. I don't want to know I'm being wheeled down the aisle."

8
TEXAS AND
BILLY MARTIN

I was as happy about getting back into baseball as I was about getting out of the rehab center. Red Dwyer was a lifesaver. He had bought this team down in South Carolina in Class A, and it was going to be a co-op team. Most of the players would be associated with the St. Louis Cardinals, but others would have ties with Atlanta, Detroit, and other big league teams.

It was to be my first shot at managing a team, and I was really excited about it. When Red talked to me, I told him that I'd never managed before but I sure as hell would like to give it a shot.

By the time I linked up with the Orangeburg team, spring training was already over. And when I got a look at the team, I knew I had a bunch of guys who just weren't good enough to be professional baseball players. They were not going to make the major leagues. Most of them were getting their last shot at the game. And that was as far as they were going to get.

THE TRUTH HURTS

On the other hand, it gave me a wonderful opportunity to learn a lot more about baseball than I ever had in my life. Suddenly I was responsible for these kids at nine different positions. I'd been an outfielder. Now I had to work with infielders, catchers, pitchers—everybody. I had to study each position and how each kid was playing it. I'd watch each one, and I'd find little things that I felt I could help them with—sometimes it was in regard to hitting, others in regard to fielding or where to play a particular type of hitter. I'd keep notes on each kid at each position, and at night I'd go home and jot them down in logbooks I kept. I really wanted to help them, but I knew I was working within definite limits. I could help some, but I knew I couldn't make them into major league baseball players.

I had a bunch of young pitchers who could not get the ball over the plate. I had a catcher playing first base. I had a shortstop who could throw the ball like a bullet, but he couldn't throw it straight to first base. I told the first baseman, "Stand somewhere down the line; maybe then he'll throw it toward the base." The only one I had in the infield who was any good was a third baseman, and they brought him up to the Double A before he could do anything for us.

The best ball player we had was an outfielder, Tito Landrum, who eventually made it to the Cardinals in 1980. He was just a kid when he played for us at Orangeburg, but he was the most well-mannered kid I think I've ever run into. His father was a career military man, and maybe that's where he got it. He really worked hard, could run, could slide, could throw the ball. I thought if any of them were going to make it, it would be him.

Tito hit a home run in the playoffs in 1983 for the Baltimore Orioles. It was in the 10th inning off Britt Burns, and it beat the White Sox. I was happy as hell, having by then had all my problems with the White Sox owners. As I watched him run around the bases, I felt just like he'd done it for me. I sent him a telegram after it and said that it was a long way from Orangeburg, South Carolina, where we had 200 people in the stands, to the American League playoffs.

Managing was some kind of new experience for me, but it felt great to be back in baseball. I'd gone down to Orangeburg by myself, and I stayed with Red Dwyer in his home there. He let me drive his jeep to get around. It was altogether a decent deal for me.

We had a bus to get the team around with, but it was virtually falling apart. I mean it was downright dangerous. So I asked Red about getting some station wagons instead. He worked something out with a dealer down there, and we got four of them. None of our games were too far away, and we ordinarily would come home at night after each away game. I had it set up so that the kid who didn't play well or made a bunch of mental mistakes would have to ride in the same station wagon with me. They all hated that because they couldn't listen to their music and instead had to listen to the Cardinals game and, of course, to me. But it got so that every night *they* knew who should be in my station wagon. I didn't have to tell them.

I really worked with those kids. And we got some results. They didn't seem to know what the hell a relay was before I got there, but halfway through the season they had relays down. They had that particular thing down as well as some of the teams in the big leagues. But we didn't win a lot of games. We had some high points, though. We knocked Charleston out of the playoffs, I remember, beating them four out of five games at the end of the season. That was satisfying to me.

Besides having a rather piss-poor team, my other big problem was myself. I got thrown out of 23 games that year, which I believe was a record in that league. The umpires there were really unbelievable. I mean they couldn't umpire in a kiddie league. They didn't just make mistakes; they didn't know what they were doing. They were so bad that I couldn't stand it. And I guess they couldn't stand me, judging from the number of games I got heaved out of. Most of them were schoolteachers or bus drivers or something like that, and this was their pastime. God, they were awful.

We finished last that year, but we had fun. After the season I took each kid aside and talked to him. I explained to him about his ability, most of them about their limited abilities. I told them honestly what I thought. And the truth of it was that I didn't think they would do any better than Class AA ball. The majority would be better off finding another way to make a living, I told them. "If you stay around," I said, "you'll be nothing but minor league bums." One mother called me and was hot as hell at me for telling her kid that.

"Ma'am," I said, "I'm just trying to tell the truth. If he feels he can still do it, he can go ahead and try. I'm not telling him to quit. I'm just giving him a tip that maybe he shouldn't waste his time since he's probably not going to make it. I may be wrong, but I doubt it very much." And I hung up on her.

When it was all over, the players chipped in and got me a golf shirt, a red and white one, which I still have to this day. It was one of the nicest presents I ever received. But I was not going to be back there the next year. So it was out to look for a job again.

I went to the World Series that year, 1973. It was between Finley's Oakland As and the New York Mets. While I was up in New York, I ran into Billy Martin, who had taken over managing the Texas Rangers that year. They were a last-place team, and he'd taken over after Whitey Herzog left.

I said to him, "Bill, I'm looking for a job. I'll take anything. I just want to be in baseball."

He knew what I was talking about, how I felt. He shook his head and said he would see what he could do. He got together with two other friends of ours, Frank Lucchesi and Kenny Aspromonte, and they tried to dig up something for me. Well, while the series was still going on, here came Billy back to me. "How would you like to have a job in group ticket sales in Texas? I can get you one for $15,000 a year working for Bob Short down there in Dallas." Billy has always had a heart of gold, and he truly was a loyal friend. I had just wanted some advice or to have him keep his ears open in case something popped up somewhere, but he went right out and lined up a job for me.

It wasn't very much money, but hell, I wanted the job. As I've always said, you take what you can get and then work your ass off at it. So I thanked Martin and took the job.

Bob Short owned the Rangers franchise, and it was in pretty poor shape. They were losers, and they were not getting a helluva lot of people to come into the ballpark and watch them get beaten. The year before, they had drawn only 650,000.

So I got right into it. I started to work really hard; in fact, before the season even started I'd made more than 50 guest appearances and set up a lot of different promotions to sell tickets to groups. I worked up a lot of different promotions. I came up with the idea to give away autographed baseballs. I got big companies down there to sponsor and underwrite things like Bat Day, when bats would be given to the first thousand kids. They'd never done things like that in Texas before.

I also got fired before the season even opened. Twice.

The first time was just after the football season had ended and I was giving a talk at the Lions Club in downtown Dallas. There was a question-and-answer period, and somebody in the audience asked, "Jimmy, what do you think about the amount of press the Texas Rangers are getting?"

115

THE TRUTH HURTS

Well, they were not getting all that much at the time. So I said, "Now that the football season is over, I think we could get better coverage than we're getting." It's what I added after that that got me in trouble, a comment about this one sportswriter with one of the Dallas newspapers. "The one thing that gets me," I said, "is that I don't know what that little Jewish guy is writing about. I don't understand his writing. He's so negative about the team all the time."

Word travels fast in Texas. When I got back to my office I got a call from the editor of the Dallas newspaper, and he was really hot. He gave me hell on the phone. "Why are you getting on the Jewish people?" he yelled at me.

"I'm not getting on the Jewish people," I said. "I'm getting on your writer, that's all. I'm getting on him because he's always so goddam negative."

"You referred to him as 'this little Jewish guy,' didn't you?"

"Isn't he Jewish? All I said was he was Jewish." I tried to explain that I didn't mean anything by it. I just didn't like the way the jerk was writing. The truth of the matter was that I couldn't remember the little jerk's name, and I just said "Jewish" so as to identify him. I didn't mean anything derogatory. Well, he kept going on and on about the Jewish thing, and I finally said, "Kiss my ass," and hung up on him.

A little while later I got a call from Bob Short, and he told me I was fired.

The next thing I got was a call from Billy Martin. He heard about my getting fired, and he called to tell me that he was very upset about it. He knew I didn't mean anything by the remark; he knew it was just me, my way of saying something. He said something like, "Well, if you go, I go."

I said, "Bill, don't be silly. I'll find another job. I love you, pal, but it ain't worth it." Billy was tremendously important to that ball club. Well, he said that, nevertheless, he was going to talk to Short about it.

The next thing I knew, I got another call, this one to tell me the organization was going to give me one more chance. I was rehired.

Then, just before the season opener, I had a run-in with another writer. He blasted me, got all over my tail about what appeared in an article in the Dallas Chamber of Commerce magazine. I'd been interviewed for the article, and it was a pretty good one as it turned out, but this guy was hot about some of the things I had said about all sportswriters. I said that 90 percent of them had no idea of what was going on on the playing field. They had no idea of a ball player's feelings out there. They did not know what it was like to go out and strike out with the bases loaded, for example, or to make an error, throw a wild pitch, that sort of thing. But then to read the things they'd write, you'd think they knew all about it. They were in some kind of fantasy world, I said.

Well, this one writer from one of the Dallas newspapers made a very big thing of it. He came up to me in the hospitality room at the stadium and started to get all over me about it. I mean he was really telling me off. So I finally told him to fuck off. I didn't hit him or anything, just yelled at him. I think I called him a little cocksucker. Well, there was a woman in there, and she went to Bob Short and told him about the incident and what I'd called the guy.

The next thing I knew, Short dragged me to a board of directors' meeting, talked about what had happened, and then fired me again.

While all this was going on, Short was also trying to sell the ball club. So I got a call from a guy who was interested in buying it, Brad Corbett. He asked me to come to his office the next day and talk to him. Brad was 34 at the time, a millionaire from the pipe business he owned. I went, and the first thing he asked me was, "What's the ball club worth?"

"Well, they've got a great farm system," I said. "In fact, they've got some of the best-looking talent I've ever seen in

117

a minor league system. And that's very valuable." I also told him that Short was desperate to sell the team and that the rumor that he was also negotiating with somebody from Houston was a lot of bullshit. We talked about the fact that Short had sold the television and radio rights to the city of Arlington, Texas, to pay off some of his debts. Corbett would not be able to get those back for something like five years. I said I thought Corbett could get the whole thing for six million dollars. He called in his lawyers, and he was anxious as a little kid. He said, "Tell 'em, Jim. Tell 'em."

Well, he bought the club, but he paid nine and a half million for it. That was the worst deal for any owner that I've heard of in my life. In 1974, you could pick up a last-place club for six million, and that's what the Rangers were. The year before, they had finished last in the American League West. They had the worst record in all baseball, 57 and 105. They didn't have a pitcher who won 10 games or a batter in the regular lineup who hit above .285. In addition, their ballpark didn't hold that many people, and it needed a lot of work. They didn't even have a sign on the stadium that said "Texas Rangers."

After he bought the club, Corbett gave me a job, the third time that year I was hired by the Rangers. I was to function as a kind of assistant to him. He also wanted me to get involved with his pipe company, act as a kind of goodwill ambassador. He wanted me to do some of its public relations work, call on its distributors, and then go with the distributors and call on the key accounts all over the country.

Corbett loved baseball, and he especially liked to talk about it. He felt he really knew it because he claimed that he played in the minor leagues. We talked baseball all the time. But he never listened to me. Still, he was a helluva nice guy. And he said to me, "You've got a job with us as long as you don't lie or steal!"

Even so, I toned down my act. I mean I watched what I said and did, a lot different from what I had been like under Short.

The Rangers were a helluva lot better in 1974 under Martin. They ended up in second place in the American League West, won 84 games and lost 76, and were only five games behind the Oakland As. They had acquired Fergie Jenkins from the Chicago Cubs, and he won 25 games for them. Jeff Burroughs was a great outfielder for them, too; he was only 23 and won the MVP award that year—25 homers, 118 RBIs, a .301 average. Mike Hargrove, their first baseman, hit .323; and Lenny Randle, who played everywhere for them, batted .302. And Jim Bibby won 19 games.

As part of the deal in getting the job, I had to go to see a psychiatrist. Bobby Brown, who was a good friend of mine and had played third base for the New York Yankees in the late 1940s and early '50s and was now a physician, a heart specialist, was on the Rangers' board of directors, and he recommended to Corbett that I do it. He wanted to be sure that I could get along with people. So I went to this psychiatrist, and, after seeing him a number of times, I felt I wasn't getting anywhere. Finally, I just asked him, "Hey, how can I get along with people better now?"

Then he'd say, "Well, what do you think, Jim?"

And I'd ask, "How can I do better with my job?"

And he'd say, "Well, what do you think, Jim?"

I said, "I didn't ask what *I* think."

All he did was sit there and take notes and punch the buttons on his tape recorder. But finally he did one very good thing. He suggested I try taking lithium. I didn't know what it was, and he told me that it was a salt additive and in my system it might strike just the right balance and I'd get on better with people and things like that.

I said, "Will that make Corbett happy?" He said he thought it would and that he'd talk to him about it. Well, after about a month on lithium, I could see that it was

119

working. I could feel that it was good for me, that I wouldn't go to extremes in my feelings, wouldn't get down so quickly. And Corbett and Bobby Brown seemed pleased. It did strike the proper chemical balance in my system, and it's been a big help to me ever since.

Then I found out that my biggest problem at the moment was physical. I was doing some PR work for Corbett's pipe company in Richmond, Virginia, and I stopped by to see Clint Courtney, who was then managing the minor league team there. Clint was an old friend. He was a helluva catcher in the days when I played. He was all over the American League—played with the Yankees, St. Louis Browns, Baltimore Orioles, White Sox, Senators, Kansas City. We had a nice visit, and then the next day I picked up the newspaper and read that he had died of a heart attack.

It really shook me up. He seemed in fine health when I talked with him. How could something like that happen so suddenly to a guy, I thought.

When I got back to Texas, I talked to Bobby Brown about it. He was a specialist in heart problems. I asked him, "How do you check your heart so something like that doesn't happen to you?" He told me the best way was a stress test, where you run on a treadmill and they measure your heart rate while you're exercising. They wire you up, and as the physical stress builds, they can determine how your heart and circulatory system are functioning.

So I did it. When he got the results he called me and had me come in. He asked me if I had had any kinds of problems regarding my heart before. I told him that I hadn't. I just wanted it checked because of what had happened to Courtney. He told me that the arteries to my heart were partially blocked, somewhere around 60 percent, he said, and that was not good. To be sure, he wanted to do another test, a catheterization. I said okay, and that was awful. That's where they send this tube into your arteries. You're not knocked out, and it is just terrible. The results from it were not good either.

Piersall reacts to some hecklers during his first year with the Washington Senators.

Close call. Lousy decision. Piersall is out in this 1962 game. The
Yankee third baseman tagging him out is Clete Boyer; the demon-
strative umpire is Joe Paparella.

Reacting to an umpire in Minnesota. Piersall, with the Senators in 1962, wants the last word after being ejected from the game.

With the now quite old "perfessor," Casey Stengel, in the New York
Mets clubhouse.

Show business in the Big Apple. Piersall doffs his cap after a most unorthodox advance from second to third—he ran backward. It was an intracity game between the Mets and the Yankees. The bemused Yankee is third baseman Clete Boyer.

Beating Mr. Cub, Ernie Banks, to a base.

The 100th home run. Piersall runs around the bases backward.

An unorthodox lead-off, Piersall turns his back to homeplate and stares
down a smiling Vic Power, first baseman for the Minnesota Twins.

In Los Angeles and admiring the famous whiskers of Gabby Hayes.

Did I clown around? Sometimes.

A bewigged Jimmy Piersall is chauffeured to home plate, accompanied by Keystone Kops. It was "Slapstick Day at the Ballpark" in Anaheim during Piersall's California Angels days.

Who says only Babe Ruth can call his shot? The White Sox catcher is J.C. Martin. Piersall did not hit a home run on the next pitch, but he did hit a single.

In the Chicago White Sox broadcast booth with fellow announcer
Harry Caray.

Jim and Jan Piersall.

Reunion of one of the Red Sox's finest outfields: Piersall, Ted Williams, and Jackie Jensen, at an old-timers' game shortly before Jensen's death.

Cronin: Fighting Fans Are Courts' Problem

By Dick Young

Jimmy Piersall's cry to arms for all ballplayers, urging them to follow his lead by popping any fan who runs onto the playing field, yesterday received a cool reception from AL prexy Joe Cronin, a pacifist.

Piersall, after decking one field invader with a left hook, and place-kicking another in the pants during a wild scene at Yankee Stadium Sunday, had said he believes all players should react similarly. "That's the only way to stop this stuff," reasoned the emotional Indian outfielder.

NOT SO, SAYS CRONIN. "I don't think Jimmy's suggestion is the answer to the problem," stated Cronin via phone from AL headquarters in Boston "After all, such a challenge might encourage a few light-heavyweights, trying to get a reputation for themselves, to run onto the field and look for a fight—and some of them might be a little better at that sort of thing than the player is."

Cronin said he believes the only solution to the roving fan nuisance is "stern action by the courts."

"If they fine violators, and throw them in jail for a few days, we may be able to stop this foolishness," he said.

CRONIN ADDED THAT PIERSALL was well within his rights, on this particular occasion. "He had to protect himself," Cronin said.

The AL prexy has not spoken to Piersall since the incident, regarding Jimmy's announced crusade of force, but indicated he intends to. "I haven't been able to get in touch with him," said Cronin, "because the Cleveland club has been traveling."

Fair Warning

—By Stark

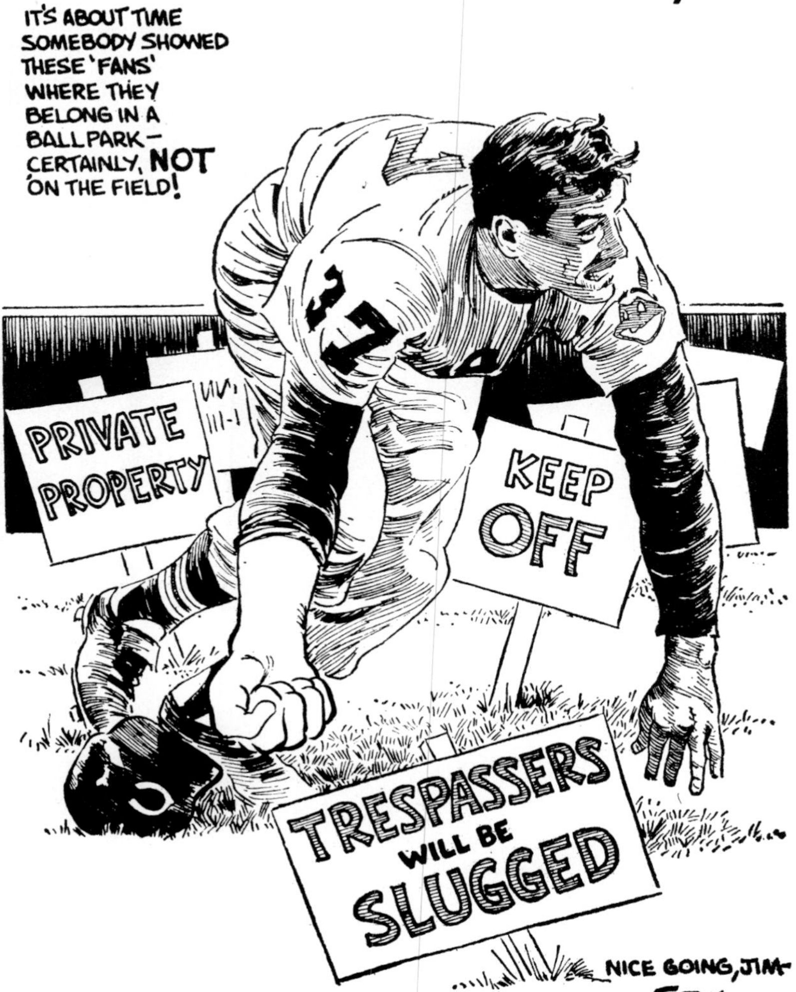

Jimmy Piersall today.

Bobby told me I had a definite heart problem. It was probably caused from stress and heredity—my father had died of a heart attack. He suggested major heart surgery, a bypass.

I said that, before I went through something like that, I wanted to check with some other doctors. Not that I didn't trust Bobby, but it was a major thing, and I wanted to be very sure. Well, they sent their findings to a couple of doctors in Cleveland, who checked it out. They came back and suggested we wait a year and then run through the tests again.

This was a pretty down time for me, obviously. Around that same time, too, my wife went back to Virginia. She couldn't take it down there in Texas, so she packed up and left. We remained separated from that point on, although we did get together on occasion to go someplace together or do something together, but we never really lived together again.

I went back to work for Corbett. It was around that time that things started to go bad for his business, and that affected his outlook on everything. Things were not going well for the ball club either. After having such a good year in 1974, the players were just not performing. Burroughs ended up hitting .226, and Fergie Jenkins lost 18 games. Only Hargrove hit above .300 and just barely (.303). It was driving Billy Martin nuts.

At spring training that year, Billy had me working with the outfielders. And I really enjoyed working as a coach. But while I was doing that, I saw the problems developing. We were not winning, and the tension around there was building all the time. They used to have me go out and golf in the morning with Billy in the hope of getting him to relax a little.

I began hearing things from Corbett and Dan O'Brien, the club's general manager. They were complaining that Billy wasn't going to meetings, that he wouldn't cooperate with them. They were saying things like there was something wrong with him. I could see what was happening. So one morning I said to him as we were golfing, "Billy, I've got to tell you. I think they're going to fire you."

"Fuck 'em," he said.

And that was his attitude at that point. He felt they weren't cooperating with him. When he tried to get things done through O'Brien, it never worked. It was not a friendly atmosphere that year.

A little while later there was a meeting, which I was at, and the thing came to a head. Corbett said to me, "What's the matter with Billy?"

I said, "The players aren't playing well. I think he may be a little tired, physically and mentally." I knew what they were up to. I said, "Why don't you give him a leave of absence for a little while?"

Their minds were already made up, however. Corbett asked me to leave the meeting then, and while I was gone they agreed to fire Billy. His record when he left was 44 and 51, a big disappointment from the year before. But he was on his way to the Yankees and a couple of World Series. Texas's loss was New York's gain.

They had another meeting then about whom to hire to replace him. I was back at that one. They were talking about trying to get Tommy Lasorda—at that time he was a coach with the Los Angeles Dodgers—or Alex Grammas, who was also coaching in the National League then.

I said, "Why the hell are you looking for somebody in that league? We're in the American League. I think it would make more sense to get somebody familiar with the teams in our league."

And surprise of surprises, they agreed with me.

Then I said, "Why don't you let Frank Lucchesi finish the season up?" He was our third base coach, and he was a very conscientious guy. I told them I thought he deserved the chance and that he would do a good job for them.

Again they agreed that it was a good idea. I couldn't believe it. I think that was the only time Corbett ever really listened to me. And Lucchesi did do a decent job for them: won 35 and lost only 32 during the remainder of that season.

After Lucchesi was hired, Billy thought that maybe he was the one who got him fired in the first place. I told him that wasn't so. "You got yourself fired," I said. "You wouldn't go to their meetings; you wouldn't cater to them a little. That's what got you canned." Believe me, I knew enough about getting fired. I was a real pro in that regard.

Lucchesi then came to me and told me that he wanted me to coach at third base for him.

"I don't want it," I said to him. And I didn't. But he talked me into it. I did it, and it went pretty well, but I was getting too keyed up by it. I would get too involved, and the stress was really getting to me. I couldn't get my mind off it. Finally I said, "I can't do this anymore." And I didn't.

When the season was over I went swimming one day in the pool at the Fontainebleau Hotel in Miami, and all of a sudden I found it a huge chore. I didn't seem to have any strength. I wasn't getting anywhere. It scared the hell out of me. I wasn't that old, after all; hell, I was only 45.

It was the heart. The blockage in the arteries had gotten worse, about 90 percent now, I was told. Bobby Brown said that I definitely had to have the heart surgery, or I would be a dead man.

I remember the night I was supposed to check into the hospital. It was awful. What a scary thing. Here they were going to operate on my heart. I was due to check in at seven o'clock. I got there, but I didn't go in. I just drove around for about four hours. I didn't want to go through with it, but I knew I had to. It's a terrible feeling when you have to face something like that. You just wish that things would change, that it was all just a bad dream, that it wasn't really happening to you. But it was. About eleven o'clock I checked in. I told the doctor on duty, "I want a shot, bang, knock me out. When I wake up in the morning I want another shot, bang. I don't want to be awake. I don't want to see anybody. I don't want to know I'm being wheeled down the aisle."

He did. When I finally woke up, the first thing I saw was this doctor leaning over me. There was a tube in my mouth, running down into me, and I grabbed at it and tried to pull it out. I guess I was moving around a lot because I heard him say, "He's all right. But give him a shot before he breaks this bed apart."

I was okay. But let me tell you, after it was over, I knew I'd gone through something terrible.

When I got out of the hospital, Corbett insisted that I move into his house. He got me set up in the guest's quarters. The maids and all the help waited on me like crazy. It was very nice. All the people around there were especially nice to me.

I was back with the team in 1976. I was doing promotional work for them and some broadcasting. Frank Lucchesi got the nod to continue as manager. But things did not go that well with the team. We did not have a .500 season and were tied for fourth place when it ended. Things were not going well with the pipe business either.

After the season, Corbett decided he didn't need me anymore. He had Dan O'Brien let me go. But it turned out to be a break for me.

In 1976, I had been doing some guest shots on the radio with Harry Caray, the White Sox announcer, when Chicago came to Texas to play the Rangers. And they had gone pretty well. I kidded Harry a lot, and he kidded me back. The people liked it, and so did Harry.

After I got the heave from the Rangers, Harry talked to Charlie Warner, who was the head of WMAQ in Chicago, about hiring me full-time to work with him on all the White Sox games. They offered me a job, a new career really, and I grabbed it. So I left Texas and headed up to Chicago and what would turn out to be one whole helluva lot of turmoil.

I said on the air, "Boy, it's cold out here tonight. . . ." The next day, when I walked into the Bard's Room, I heard, "Hey, Piersall, come over here, I want to talk to you." [Bill] Veeck looked me straight in the eye and said, "It's never cold at the ballpark! And don't you forget it."

9
A NEW CAREER

I got an indication of what my Chicago years were going to be like the day I arrived from Texas for the press conference to announce that I would be working with Harry Caray. It was the same day that Mayor Daley died— Richard J. Daley, a legend in Chicago. Needless to say, my press conference was not uppermost in the minds of the media people or the writers. My debut, one might say, was star-crossed.

I hadn't really thought that I was going to get the job in the first place. I wanted it. In fact, once I knew they were interested, I'd campaigned for it. Charlie Warner of WMAQ radio wanted me, I knew, but the contract offer was continually being put off. Ed Morris of Channel 44, the general manager of the television station that broadcast the White Sox games, seemed interested, too. The hang-up was with Bill Veeck, who controlled the White Sox.

Finally they brought me up to Chicago. I remember it vividly. It was a sunny day but cold as hell—five below zero, I think it was. Charlie Warner picked me up, and we drove in his van over to Bill Veeck's apartment. Bill wasn't feeling too good that day, and he paid very little attention to me. His reception was not overwhelmingly warm. I sat there and listened as Charlie did all the talking, trying to sell Veeck on me as Harry's sidekick. I had this gnawing feeling that Veeck did not want to hire me, in fact was not too thrilled even to see me there. I don't know whether he was thinking about the time in 1959 when I threw the baseball at his sacred scoreboard or not. If he was, I was sure I wouldn't get the job.

Veeck listened to Charlie and continued to ignore me. I finally said to myself, "Hey, what the hell is this? Why am I here? He doesn't want me."

Then, out of the blue, Veeck turned to me and said, "Well, we don't have very much money; all we can afford is $35,000 for the year."

Before I could blink, I said. "I'll take it!" Hell, it was $15,000 more than I'd been making in Texas, and here I was unemployed.

So, in 1977, I had a brand-new career.

There were a lot of worries that went along with it, however. First, I didn't really know if I could work with Harry Caray on a regular basis. After all, up to that time, Harry had worked pretty much alone. We'd worked well together down in Texas, but those were just guest shots and not a full-time color job. And I had never worked as a regular announcer. I'd done bits and pieces in California and Texas, but I'd never worked as a regular announcer every day. I had no way of knowing whether or not I could do it. I knew that I understood baseball and that I wasn't afraid to tell it like I saw it. But I didn't know how it would all come out once I was on the air. It was scary.

I also didn't know much about Chicago. I'd been there, of course, when I played, but then I just got on the bus and went from the hotel to the ballpark and back. I'd heard all the stories about the crime and killings, Al Capone stuff, just like everybody else had heard about Chicago. I knew it was a damn big town, cold as hell, and probably unfriendly. I'd been used to places like Roanoke, Virginia, and Fort Worth, Texas, lately. I liked the open space, the quiet; it wasn't going to be like that in Chicago, I knew.

Anyway, nobody paid much attention to my formal arrival; they were all too taken up with Mayor Daley's formal departure.

I got together with Harry, and he was very nice when I first got to town. I said to him, "Harry, I'm going to need your help because there's a lot about this business I don't know."

He said, "Don't worry, kid; we'll have fun. Glad to have you with us." That was the way Harry was.

And Chicago wasn't bad. I didn't see anybody killed or mugged on the street. The people I met, it turned out, were friendly and nice to be around. One of them, Mel Gorlick, a businessman, helped me find a place to live where it was quiet and peaceful, a suburb called Woodridge, which was only about 25 minutes from Comiskey Park by way of one of the expressways.

My contract was for one year. "Be yourself," Harry told me. And, of course, I was. I really broke in, so to speak, down at spring training in Sarasota, Florida. I worked with Harry, and things went pretty well from the start. I also worked with a female announcer, Mary Shane, who was good, knew sports, was a true baseball fan, and turned out to be a terrific help to me. If a woman ever could have made it as a big-time baseball announcer, it was Mary. She had all that it takes in terms of knowledge and quick reactions, but she lacked experience, and some people didn't like her voice on the radio.

Mary and I went all over together down there to do the spring training games. She'd do the play-by-play, and I'd do the color, then we'd switch and I'd do the play-by-play and she'd do the color. I was terrible at first doing the play-by-play. It just wasn't my bag. I knew that I could explain the game, which is doing the color, but play-by-play was a different animal altogether. You just don't walk in and start doing it. It takes a lot of experience to do it well. Mary didn't make it through the regular season because she didn't have a name, she wasn't established, and the producers were concerned about her voice, and that was her downfall.

We opened the 1977 season in Toronto. It was snowing, and it was cold. Harry always worked with the windows open, even on a day like that. We didn't think they'd play the game. The ball players lined up before the game and were playing football with a baseball. But they played it anyway. And I froze my ass off up in the broadcast booth.

After the game, I had to go down on the field to do an interview. It was the first of about 800 that I would do over the next four years. The White Sox lost to the Blue Jays that day, so I was going to interview the winning pitcher, Jerry Garvin. He was a rookie that year, 21 years old, and had pitched a pretty good game. He had great moves to first and second base.

Tommy Harmon, the famous football player from Michigan who later became a great announcer, had told me, "When you do an interview, always play off the person you're interviewing." Great advice. I had it in mind when I got Garvin up there. "You have a really good move to first base. How did you develop it?" I asked.

"I learned it in high school," he said. Then silence. That was about the longest answer I got during the entire interview. I finally started asking him about his mother because I couldn't get anything out of him about baseball or the game that he had just pitched. So I ended up doing all the talking. It was an awful way to start. I was down there, knew it was going badly, and up in the press box they were giving me a sign to stretch the interview out.

They needed to fill more time on the air with it. The next 799 interviews were much better.

Harry had a lot of patience with me. There were times when I was talking too much, other times when I was coming in with the color when I shouldn't have, things like that. And when I did that kind of thing he'd point it out and tell me why I shouldn't be doing it. "When you say something, be sure you have something to say," he'd tell me. Or, "Don't repeat things I just said. You don't want to do the play-by-play again."

I liked Harry very much for all his patience and help in those days.

The only thing I didn't like about Harry was his driving. God, he was the lousiest driver in the world. First of all, he was color-blind. And second, he seldom paid attention to what was going on around him when he was driving. I remember one instance. We were late going out to a game one day in Florida. I was in the back seat, and Lorn Brown, one of our other announcers, was up front with Harry. I never wanted to sit in the suicide seat with Harry driving. Anyway, there was a big milk truck going through the intersection ahead of us, and Harry paid no attention to it, kept right on going and drove up on the sidewalk to avoid hitting the milk truck, and then just drove off it on his way, as if nothing had happened.

But as an announcer, Harry was a true pro. He was always prepared when he went into the booth. He was a great salesman for the ball club and for the program's sponsors. And he could be witty. Harry was always loyal to me when things got a little sticky. And that, of course, happened a lot.

I got myself involved with controversy from the beginning. The problem, basically, was that I would tell it the way I saw it. I'd get very enthused during a ball game because I loved the game itself. And I knew the game. When a guy made a bad play, I could see it and I'd say he made a bad play. I'd *describe* the play he made, and if it was a bad one, obviously that's how it would come out. Or if he didn't hustle or he made a mental mistake, I told what he did.

There was one thing that I did that was wrong, however. I was repetitious. Ed Morris of Channel 44 pointed that out to me. "Don't keep bringing up a bad play," he said. "Once you've said it, let it drop. Don't bother bringing it up later in the game." I didn't always follow that advice, but I know it was right.

When a player did something wrong, I didn't care whether he was on the White Sox, the Yankees, the Rangers, or the Brewers. And I wasn't trying to hurt the ball players. I was trying to report to the fans what happened and why I felt it happened. The ball player's name didn't mean anything to me. What he did was my concern. Hell, the fans in the grandstands could tell, and they didn't cheer for a White Sox player when he goofed up. They wouldn't ignore it. They'd yell or boo.

A guy who summed up my brand of broadcasting best, I felt, was Jim Murray of the *Los Angeles Times*, one of the most famous sportswriters around. He wrote this about it later:

> Play-by-play baseball announcers are in the employ of teams they purport to "cover." It's a form of enlightened press agentry.
>
> Protocol therefore calls for a leavening of journalistic acuity. The home team has no warts on it. They are the guys in the white hats. And uniforms. When they pop it up, they "just got under it a little bit." Their pitcher is never wild, the mound is just too high. Their hitters are not being fooled, they're "overanxious."
>
> Crowds in other towns are "mobs," as in "unruly." The home fans are just "enthusiastic," indulging in some "good-natured" ribbing.
>
> Visiting base runners are "thugs" when they barrel

into infielders to break up the double play. It's "uncalled
for." Ours are just "playing the game the way it's meant
to be played."

Our team "hasn't put it together yet," theirs is in a
"slump." Our team is "wracked with injuries," theirs is
"playing over their heads." Our team makes "marvelous!" plays, theirs has balls "hit right at them." Our team
makes "human errors," theirs are just "poor fielders."

Above all, you are deferential to top management.
"Minister" is the proper form of address for the owner.
And, you never, never refer to his wife as "a bore."

Into this idyllic gentlemen's club, a society of rose-col-
ored tonsils, strode James Anthony Piersall not so many
years ago. Now, James sees things precisely as they are,
not as they should be. An outstanding centerfielder in his
day, he gets a good jump on the ball in life, too.

When James was hired to do color work on the Chicago White Sox broadcasts, he never caught on there
were two sets of values out there, one for "us," and one
for "them." Jimmy thought when a player made a gaffe,
it didn't matter what color his uniform was. Jimmy also
thought he "had a right to his own opinion."

In 1977, the White Sox actually had a good team. They
had some pretty big names out there that year: Oscar
Gamble, who hit 31 home runs, and Richie Zisk, who hit
another 30. They had Chet Lemon, Jorge Orta, and Ralph
Garr. Steve Stone was their best pitcher. Bob Lemon
managed the Sox, and they finished third in the American
League West behind Kansas City and Texas. They were 90
and 72, 12 games out. The team did well because the
players could score a lot of runs. Pitching was one of their
problems, fielding was another, but hell, they'd come back
with five runs in the eighth inning or something like that
and win the ball game. They were leading for a while in the
AL West, and they did have a good chance to win it for
some time.

Actually, that year went pretty smoothly. With the team

winning most of the time and all those home runs and big scores, the feeling around the White Sox offices was pretty good. There was some talk that I was negative. But I wasn't. As I said then when somebody would bring that up, "I don't criticize; I say what I see."

One time Bob Lemon was asked about Harry and me being tough on the Sox players and negative on the team. He said, "What Harry and Jimmy do doesn't bother me. That's the way they work, and that's their job. I do mine, and they do theirs. That's all." I often thought afterward that it would be great if every manager and every player had that attitude.

On the other hand, Bill Veeck was not all that fond of it when we would say something that he thought was negative. He would get upset. When that happened, the next day in the Bard's Room, the White Sox's hospitality room at the ballpark where Veeck would hold court at a corner table before each game, I'd hear, "Hey, Piersall, come over here. I want to talk to you." If everything had gone well and he wasn't upset, it would be, "Hey, James, come over here. I want to talk to you."

I remember one night early in the season when it was awfully cold. I said on the air, "Boy, it's cold out here tonight. I'm glad this game is over so I can go home and crawl into a nice warm bed."

The next day, when I walked into the Bard's Room, I heard, "Hey, Piersall, come over here. I want to talk to you." Veeck looked me straight in the eye and said, "It's never cold at the ballpark! And don't you forget it."

"What do you mean it's never cold?" I said. "It *was* cold out there." But I knew what he was saying. I got the message. It's just that I couldn't do that kind of thing.

When the season ended I didn't know quite what was going to happen. Harry and I had gotten along well, worked well together, and I felt he was pleased with the arrangement. The fans liked it. They knew I was outspoken, and they got a kick out of it. They liked the way Harry and I kidded with each other. Harry would say something like, "Ohhhh, that Nancy Faust can really play the organ. Don't you love it? Her music could drive me to dance."

And I'd say something like, "Your dancing could drive me to drink, Harry."

Or he would say, "Hey, Jimmy, you're all dressed up tonight. Must be because somebody's doing a story about you, eh?"

And I'd say, "I'm just glad you didn't wear your polka dot shirt, Harry. That's the ugliest shirt I've ever seen."

And when I'd really get riled up or excited during a game, he would sometimes say, "Hey, Jimmy, did you forget to take your pill today?" referring to the lithium I take. I'd tell him, "Harry, I'm the only guy around here who can prove he's okay. I've got my papers. I get them renewed every year to prove that I'm well." We had a good rapport going.

Both Charlie Warner and Ed Morris said they liked the way we worked and were pleased with us as a team. But some of the players were grousing that we got on them. And I'd had my run-ins with Bill Veeck during the year. So I didn't know whether I'd be offered a new contract. And I had to sweat it out. Normally, somebody in my position would get a contract at the end of the season, or he'd be fired. I had to wait and wait. Finally, in February of 1978, I got the contract. I got it because Ed Morris went to Bill Veeck on my behalf, and apparently he was convincing. He was a television man, and he felt I was good for the show. If it was just up to Veeck, I don't think I would have been back. So I was happy, although I was not happy at having been stalled off so long.

It was a different ball game after 1977. In 1978, the White Sox did not have a good team. Gamble and Zisk were gone; they were free agents, and Veeck said he could not afford them. Only one batter hit above .275 that year.

and that was Chet Lemon (.300). Steve Stone won 12 games, which was the most any Sox pitcher had won that season, but he also lost 12 games. Bob Lemon was fired midway through the season but not too long after was hired by George Steinbrenner to manage the Yankees. Larry Doby took over in Chicago. The problem was that Doby was not a manager. He'd done some coaching, but he was totally inexperienced as a manager. The Sox ended up with a dismal record, 71 and 90, fifth place, and 20½ games behind.

At spring training that year, Veeck asked me to work with the outfielders. I liked that idea a lot and told him that; so he added the duties of outfield coach to my job description. I worked like hell with the outfielders, really got involved. After a while, Veeck called me over to a meeting by the hotel pool where he was staying and told me he thought it was working out just fine and gave me a $5,000 raise for coaching.

The only outfielder I didn't work much with was Chet Lemon. He was the best defensive player we had in the outfield, but he had trouble charging balls back then. He was not the center fielder he is today. But he told me that he wanted to do it his way. He didn't need any help, he said, because he was already a premier center fielder. I couldn't force myself on him, so we didn't work together. But I did a lot with the others, and I was out there running with them, working out with them, hitting fungoes. I got them working together, calling for the ball, letting each other know "I got it!" I really liked it.

Up in the broadcast booth, I was as outspoken as ever. Even about the outfielders I worked with. I got on Ralph Garr about his fielding. He was a good hitter, but every time he went after a ball in the field it was an adventure. I mentioned that on the air, and both Harry and I made fun of his fielding on more than one occasion. Well, he really got upset with me. One day, before a game, he came up to me and said, "Hey, man, come here." I walked over, and he glared at me. "Didn't you ever make any errors?"

I told him that in 17 years of playing the outfield I had a career fielding average of .997, so I couldn't have made a whole helluva lot, about one a year maybe. He said, "Oh," and walked away. Garr is a really nice guy, and he was a helluva hitter. I said nice things about him as a hitter and a hustler, but I couldn't help commenting on his lousy fielding. That's the way I was, still am, and that's the way I feel the fans wanted it told.

The player with whom I had the most run-ins was Eric Soderholm, both that year and in the first part of 1979. Soderholm had bad legs, bad knees, and kept trying to get them better. I commented on his lack of speed a number of times, and he didn't like it. I would say something like, "It takes two singles to get Soderholm home from second base."

Before each season he really worked out, trying to get the legs stronger. He deserved a lot of credit for how hard he tried. And he did some other things during the season to try to improve his speed, and I had a few things to say about that. He went to a hypnotist and told the press and media about it. He'd call up this hypnotist, and the guy would put him in a trance on the telephone. I thought it was ridiculous. But I said that it was his prerogative. It was also my prerogative to say I didn't believe in it. How many guys in the Hall of Fame ever got hypnotized?

He then got on a nutrition kick and told everybody about it. Health foods and nutrition were going to make him faster. I said, "Crap." I said, "Nutrition makes me puke." He didn't like that either.

It got to him a lot about being slow, and we went back and forth in regard to it. Finally I challenged him to a race one day. I was pretty near 50 years old, I told him, just out of open heart surgery, but I'd still race him and beat him. I said I'd even race him for a thousand dollars. He said he wanted to race on a straightaway. I said, "No, let's race around the bases. That's where you're so slow, and that's where you're being paid to run." He said he wanted me to agree that if I lost I'd never say anything about his running again. Well, we never did get together. I think Veeck told him not to race against me. Anyway, Soderholm was traded to the Texas Rangers before we could get to it.

A lot of the players said I was hypercritical. So did Don Kessinger, who was the manager for most of 1979. I think the truth of the matter really was that *they* were hypersensitive. Harry and I were just reporting what we saw going on down on the playing field.

Harry said it best around that time: "You can't lie to the fans. They've got eyes. They know what's happening out there." But the players would get all upset. So would their wives—"He's saying something nasty about my husband, and my husband comes home from the ballpark, and he's all upset." Sheer crap. If he was upset, he should have been upset with what he did on the field, not the fact that Harry and I reported it.

Our duty was to the fans who watched and listened to us. And I feel sure that they were on our side. A writer for the *Chicago Sun-Times*, Mike Downey, wrote about it early in the 1979 season: "It used to be that you never knew what Jimmy Piersall would do next. Now you never know what Jimmy Piersall is going to say next. His way of speaking his mind has a way of irritating the people he's talking about. But it does not irritate most of the people *to whom* he is talking. Jimmy Piersall, the White Sox broadcaster, Harry Caray's partner, has become a popular man in the bleachers."

When something was done well, we said it. I cheered for the team. Whether the players or the manager or Bill Veeck believed it, I was a company man, just as I always had been at any job I ever had. But I was also honest. And I told the truth. And sometimes the truth hurts.

There just weren't a lot of good things to say about the White Sox in 1978 and 1979. The team finished fifth each year, wasn't even close to .500 ball. They had four different managers in those two years. What can you say about all that? Everything's terrific? It's warm at the ballpark when the temperature is 32 degrees? The guy's an Olympic sprinter when it takes him half an inning to run from first base to second? The guy is another Willie Mays when he makes two errors in the same inning?

And if I felt the players were hypersensitive, the umpires were downright paranoid. Talk about thin skins! I received a letter from a law firm in Philadelphia, which is reproduced in all its glory on the next page.

RICHARD G. PHILLIPS ASSOCIATES
ATTORNEYS AND COUNSELLORS AT LAW

May 1, 1978

Mr. James Piersall
c/o Chicago White Sox
Comiskey Park
Dan Ryan at 35th Street
Chicago, Illinois 60616

Dear Mr. Piersall:

Please be advised of our representation of the Major League
Umpire's Association.

We have received complaints that you have embarked upon a
campaign of constant personal and professional criticism of
many of the American League Umpires. Needless to say, Major
League umpires recognize that, by the nature of their jobs,
they will be subject to criticism from fans, players and
sportscasters. Moreover, the umpires recognize the privilege
of sportscasters to make fair comment upon the events of the
game. We are concerned, however, that your comments exceed
the limits of fairness.

Please be advised that we intend to investigate any further
complaints of this nature and that we stand ready to undertake
such appropriate legal action as may be necessary to protect
the interests of the Major League Umpires.

Yours very truly,

RICHARD G. PHILLIPS ASSOCIATES

BY: JOHN W. MORRIS, ESQUIRE

JWM/mrl
c.c. Bob Engel
      Dave Phillips
      Mike Veeck
      Lee MacPhail

That letter speaks for itself. You'd think we were announcing games in Nazi Germany and knocking the Gestapo.

As far as my broadcasting career went, it was the same ritual after each of those seasons as it had been after 1977. No contract, the long wait, everybody speculating whether I'd be back or not—especially me. But finally the contracts came through, and I'd be off and running again.

So the Chicago Sun-Times *took it upon themselves to conduct a poll of their readers on the subject. In the paper they ran a mail-in campaign asking the fans to vote on whether or not I should be fired. They had ads in the newspaper and posters all over town, on every newsstand. "Piersall: Should Sox Keep or Dump Him?" they said. It was unbelievable. It was as if they were trying to get me fired.*

10
CHICAGO CONTROVERSIES

In 1980, I did not exactly get off on the right foot when on a noontime television show I referred to Bill Veeck's wife, Mary Frances, as a "colossal bore."

It came about after she had said on another show, the one she had with Bill called "Mary Frances Veeck and Friend," that the kinds of things I said during a ball game were not good for the ball players. It was something to the effect that I hurt young ball players like you would crush a young plant.

That really upset me. Well, the next day I was scheduled to appear on Lee Phillip's television show. I said to my girlfriend Jan before I left for it, "I'm going to get in trouble today, I just know it." I even asked Lee Phillip before the show not to bring up what Mary Frances Veeck had said. I told her that I didn't want to talk about it. But she did bring it up, and when she did I just reacted to it. I said, "Mrs. Veeck is a colossal bore. She ought to stay in the kitchen, where she belongs. I don't know anything about the kitchen, so I don't say anything about it. She ought to be the same about baseball."

Needless to say, that statement got a lot of ink and a lot of airtime around Chicago. Bill Veeck didn't say anything to me about it, but the press made a huge thing out of it. Was I going to be fired, they were all asking. Should I be? Well, they didn't get an answer from the White Sox or the television or radio people. So the *Chicago Sun-Times* took it upon themselves to conduct a poll of their readers on the subject. In the paper they ran a mail-in campaign asking the fans to vote on whether or not I should be fired. They had ads in the newspaper and posters all over town, on every newsstand. "Piersall: Should Sox Keep or Dump Him?" they said. It was unbelievable. It was as if they were trying to get me fired.

The fans did react to it. They sent in their ballots, more than 7,000 of them, and 9 out of 10 voted that I should be kept. That was very heartwarming.

Harry Caray wrote the paper and cast a vote for keeping me. He said in the cover letter, "Only one man ever compared in interest to Piersall, and that was my first partner, the late Gabby Street. Most ex-ball-players are so deadly boring on the air: Piersall is opinionated and that's what a commentator is supposed to be." And Ed Morris of Channel 44 wrote, too: "Controversial—yes; wrong—no. Jimmy Piersall calls them as he sees them, and his opinion is an informed opinion. In an era of blandness, Piersall is refreshing. I hired him, and I back him."

The whole thing was the talk of the town for over a week. I thought about suing the newspaper for what they did. Never in my life had I heard of a newspaper polling their readers as to whether a person should be fired or kept on the job. It was a terrible week for me. I had migraine headaches. I was furious, then depressed. What if the vote went against me? Would I then be fired, out of a job? The *Sun-Times* didn't care what would happen to me.

They were using me and the possibility of getting me fired just to sell some extra newspapers. But I didn't sue them because I was told I didn't have a case. I couldn't prove "intent to hurt" me.

Looking back on it, the only thing I do regret is having said that Mary Frances Veeck was a bore. She isn't. She is and always was a very nice person. And she knew that I was popping off, reacting to what she and Bill were saying about me when I was working in the booth. When Jan and I got married later she sent us a wonderful letter wishing us well.

Nineteen eighty was also the year that Tony LaRussa got his contract with the White Sox. He had come as manager during the 1979 season to replace Don Kessinger, whom Veeck had fired. LaRussa managed the team in 54 games in 1979, and the team won half of them.

LaRussa did not have the credentials, however, to be a major league manager. There were a couple of reasons Veeck hired him, in my opinion. First, he didn't have to pay him much. Second, he felt he could manipulate him easily. Veeck always wanted to have some say in how the team was managed—who would be starting, who shouldn't be starting, things like that. So he went to the minor leagues to find a manager that he could control, and he dredged up LaRussa. The total experience that LaRussa had at that point was one year managing Knoxville in Double A and half a year with Iowa in Triple A.

At spring training in 1980, LaRussa asked me to coach the outfielders. I told him that I'd love to do it. I also worked with other players down there in Florida on their baserunning that year. There was no extra pay for coaching, but I didn't care. I just loved being an integral part of the game, and I truly believed I could be of help to the ball players.

At that point in our relationship, LaRussa and I got along fine. We talked a lot. Tony was a great one for picking

145

people's brains—coaches, other managers, guys like my-self. He had a real talent for getting things out of people that he could use to help the ball players. But as a manager then he was just beginning to learn the trade. Veeck was letting him get his basic managerial experience by han-dling the White Sox.

I told LaRussa at the outset that, if he ever felt there was a problem with me up in the press box and coaching at the same time, he should just let me know and I'd step out of the coaching job. I said that some of the ball players that I would be working with might not like what I was saying about their play when I was working upstairs. If there was a conflict of interest, I would quit the coaching.

Well, there was a lot to say about the way the White Sox were playing that year. The team stunk. Veeck had gotten a lot of pretty worthless free agents, the ones he said he could afford, and they were lousy. Most of them were eventually sent back down to the Sox farm team in Triple A, and they couldn't win there either.

I had a lot to say about the performances and the mistakes I saw on the field. As a result, in late June while we were out in California, Tony said to me that he felt it was better for the ball club if I wasn't on the field anymore. I said that was fine, that's what we had agreed upon back in spring training. I said that I'd tell the writers that I was dropping the coaching because having two jobs like that was just too much work. And, in fact, it was.

Then I found out the next morning from Rich Wortham, one of the White Sox pitchers and the player rep, that LaRussa had had a vote on the airplane on the way out there among the players as to whether I should be kept as a coach. When I heard that I said, "Hell, he didn't have to do that. All he had to do was ask me to step down. He knew that." Then I heard that Chet Lemon had a lot to do with it, that he was the one bugging LaRussa about me. He was upset because I was mentioning that the "premier" center fielder was not doing very well in the field. But, hell, everybody was criticizing him around then about that. It shouldn't have mattered to him whether I continued to coach or not because I wasn't working with him in the first place.

I don't know what the results of LaRussa's poll were, but I do know some of the players didn't like it. Wayne Nordhagen was quoted in the *Chicago Tribune* as saying, "I never got to vote on the issue." And in the *Chicago Sun-Times*, he said, "Jimmy Piersall helped me a lot. Hell, he helped all the outfielders. I hope he's back soon."

The sportswriters, however, turned the whole situation around. In the Los Angeles newspapers, they wrote that the vote was *my* idea, that I had it taken because I wanted to get a vote of confidence from the players on the field. I said that was utterly absurd.

A week later, we were back in Chicago. I was still unhappy about the sportswriters trying to make me the center of attention in what had been LaRussa's poll. It was just so wrong and stupid. Then I heard that a writer by the name of Bob Gallas for the *Arlington Heights Daily Herald*, a Chicago suburban newspaper, had been around asking the players about it. I was told that he wanted to know if it was true that I had been trying to get a vote of confidence from the players and that it had backfired and I had gotten fired as a coach instead. He was resurrecting the whole stupid story again.

It came to a head on July 2nd. I'd been out at Comiskey Park most of the day, working very hard, taping interviews and doing some pieces for the Little League clinics that Channel 44 was sponsoring. The Sox had a game that night against the California Angels which I had to work. So after we finished up the taping sessions, I went into the clubhouse and took a shower. When I got out of the shower, Greg Pryor, a White Sox infielder, came over to me and said, "Hey, you know that Gallas guy is out there asking

147

around about what happened on the vote thing out on the West Coast."

I got dressed and went out to one of the concession stands to get a couple of tacos. It was about an hour and a half before the game. Then I went back into the clubhouse to get a soft drink. At the other end of it was Gallas, talking to Ross Baumgarten, one of the Sox pitchers, and Herman Schneider, the team trainer.

When I saw him I hollered down at him, "Hey, Gallas, if you've got anything you want to know about me, ask *me*. Never mind asking the kids, they've got enough trouble just playing ball. What do you want to hear?"

He shouted something back, and I walked all the way down to where he was standing. We got into an argument and were shouting at each other and then got into a little scuffle. It took all of about three to five seconds—the scuffle, that is. Art Kusnyer, a Sox coach, pulled me away, and Herman Schneider grabbed Gallas around the neck from behind and held him. If I had wanted to hurt Gallas, I would have and could have. But I didn't. I just wanted to shake him up a little. After it, however, he went around telling everybody that I had tried to strangle him.

Later I was on my way up to the broadcast booth, and Jim Angio, who was in charge of production for Channel 44, came up to me and said, "Be careful; I hear Mike Veeck [Bill Veeck's son] is looking for you, and he's got some other guy with him. I think there could be some trouble." Then he said he would come with me, just in case. Angio was a big, strong guy, about 245 pounds.

I got into the broadcast booth and was sitting at the microphone, watching the team warm up down on the field. Angio had gone to the bathroom, and while he was there Mike Veeck came in behind me and started shouting, "You can't say things like that about my mother," referring to the time I called her a colossal bore about a month earlier. "I'll show you." And then he grabbed me around the neck from behind. He was shouting then about my scuffling with Gallas, and at the same time was dragging me backward out of the chair. I hit the base of my spine on the floor, and it hurt like hell. He was choking me bad. I couldn't breathe. I couldn't get loose either because he had me from behind. He was bananas. If Jim Angio hadn't come out of the john and, along with a couple of other guys, pulled him off, he might have killed me. If he didn't choke me to death, my heart might have gone out.

It was a terrible experience, and I was really upset. With the Gallas thing earlier and now Mike Veeck attacking me, I felt the whole world was falling apart, caving in on me. It was horrible. Finally, the security guards took me to Bill Veeck's office. Inside, with my whole world seemingly coming apart, I got into a crying jag. Bill got me to lie down on his couch. Besides the mental upset, I was also feeling bad physically. I had pains in my chest, in my shoulder, going down my arm. My heart was beating like crazy. My neck, where he had had hold of me, was throbbing. My spine was bruised and bleeding. The pressures of it all just exploded on me.

The White Sox then took me over to Illinois Masonic Hospital for some tests. The guards were terrific and calmed me down. The team physician, Dr. Sid Shafer, came to the hospital right away and spent a long time with me. It was a big help and I loved him for it.

The next day I called Gallas to apologize. The night before he had threatened to prefer charges against me but then decided against it. I told him on the telephone that I hadn't meant to hurt him, if indeed I had, and that I was sorry nonetheless. I explained that all these things had been building up inside me since the writers in California had tried to make me a heavy and look ridiculous in regard to LaRussa's player poll. Gallas accepted my apology, and then we laughed at the statement he made that was carried in the newspapers. He had gotten a number of

THE TRUTH HURTS

telephone calls from fans of mine who were sticking up for me and asking him to forget about the incident. He finally said, "I'm sorry as hell I bruised Jimmy's fingers with my throat." I thought the remark was funny—the way he put it, that is—but it was kind of ridiculous because my fingers and his throat never met.

There was, of course, a lot of speculation again that I'd be fired for sure now. It was in all the newspapers. But I also got a lot of support from people like Ed Morris, Harry Caray, even Bill Veeck. They were very understanding. "I'll fight like hell for him," Morris was quoted as saying. "He'll be back." And it was Veeck who took care of me, calmed me down in his office, and got me taken to the hospital. Harry was concerned about the pressures that I was under in the job but said publicly he hoped I could get some rest and come back on the air with him. A couple of the Chicago sportswriters, Bill Gleason of the *Sun-Times* and Bob Verdi of the *Tribune,* also went to bat for me, writing columns in which they expressed the hope that I would not be fired. Johnny Morris of CBS-TV came to visit me in the hospital. We spent more than an hour talking, and he was basically there to console, help, and offer support to me.

Morris was the first one who was allowed to talk to me in the hospital. My girlfriend Jan had come down to the hospital the night I was admitted even though I'd told her not to do it. I didn't want her to get involved; it was depressing enough for me, and I didn't want to put her through it as well. But she came because she wanted to help, and she stayed there all night—slept on the floor in my room. She kept the press away from me. She talked to them, handled the whole thing, and gave me an extraordinary amount of support and protection, which at that precise time I really needed. She was a tremendous help to me then, and it was principally through her efforts that I made a quick recovery. When I saw what she was doing for me, and how she was handling it for me, I thought that the best thing for both of us would be to get married. I thought about it as I lay there in the hospital: this is the woman I need and want. I'd been soured on marriage after two unsuccessful ones. But now I didn't feel that way anymore. And later we did get married.

I stayed in the hospital for almost a week while they ran all kinds of tests on my heart, which was showing some irregularities, and treated my back. As far as my job was concerned, I was put on what they called an "indefinite medical leave of absence." Veeck, Ed Morris of Channel 44, and Bill O'Donnell of WBBM radio issued a joint statement: "It was the considered opinion of all that Jimmy's health and well-being is of overriding importance, and to further this, it was decided that he be granted time to rest and regroup. Any further consideration of the situation will await Jimmy's complete recovery."

A lot better than "You're fired!"

But it was also limbo. I did need a rest. I did need to get away from the pressures. I knew that. Veeck, Morris, and O'Donnell also wanted me to go down to Texas and see the psychiatrist who had treated me before and also Bobby Brown in regard to my heart. So I went there.

I sat down with the psychiatrist and told him, "You know my fate is in your hands. If you tell them that I'm not capable of going back on the air, I'm dead." And that, of course, was true. Then I told him, "I'm not any different than I was before. I'm just a little tired now, in need of a little rest. I scuffled with a guy up there in Chicago, but that doesn't mean I'm nuts. Anybody else blows his stack, nobody goes around saying he's crazy." I explained to him that I would never change, that I was independent, a nonconformist, that I always had been and always would be. I told him that I had not been taking the lithium as regularly as I should have and that, along with the increasing pressures, had simply gotten to me. I knew that. Now I wanted him to understand it because wherever I was

THE TRUTH HURTS

going would be determined by his comprehension of that. As it turned out, both he and Bobby Brown gave me a clean bill of health.

While this was going on, I was getting a helluva lot of support in Chicago. The fans called the television station, the radio station, the White Sox, asking that I be put back on the air. They estimated there were a thousand calls in all. And I got almost 4,000 letters, which I felt was downright incredible. At the ball park, they had banners—"We Want Jimmy," "Bring Piersall Back," that kind of thing. They would yell the same kinds of things up to Harry in the broadcast booth. It really meant a great deal to me.

The decision was finally made to put me back on the air. They also felt it would be better for me and perhaps cause less of a to-do if I came back while the club was on the road. It was two weeks after the incidents with Gallas and Mike Veeck, and the Sox were playing the Rangers down in Texas when I came back on the air. I was really glad to be back.

One of the first statements I made was to thank the fans for all their support. "Through a tough time," I said, "you were there. Hundreds of telephone calls, letters, support at the ball park, I'll never forget that for the rest of my life."

Harry said on the air, "I missed you. I never worked so hard in my life. One night I almost called you up in the hospital and asked you to move over." The way Harry received me back was terrific. To me, the definition of a friend is someone who, when you're really down, is truly loyal to you and simply wants to help you, and that's what Harry Caray was to me.

Everything was back to normal after that. The White Sox continued to stink up the American League West. They gave Harry and me a lot to talk about. The Sox ended up with a record of 70 and 90 that year, fifth place and 26 games behind.

When it was over, I didn't know whether I'd be back in

the booth or not. I suspected maybe I might not when Bill Veeck asked me if I'd like to be a scout for the team, said he'd pay me $35,000 a year.

The White Sox, however, were for sale around that time. It looked like Edward DeBartolo, a multimillionaire who built shopping centers, was going to buy it. I was brought out to meet him during one of his trips to Chicago. Nick Kladis, who owned part of the White Sox along with Veeck and who had been a great basketball player at Loyola University in Chicago, was the man who introduced us and set up the meeting. I had lunch with DeBartolo, and he implied that I could be nicely involved with the organization if he indeed got the team.

But DeBartolo didn't get the White Sox. The commissioner of baseball, Bowie Kuhn, and some of the other American League team owners would not approve the sale to him. I could never understand that. It was a shady deal at worst and hypocritical at best. The reason, they said, was because DeBartolo was involved with the racetracks, had investments in one or something like that. Well, that was absurd. Hell, George Steinbrenner, who owned the Yankees, and John Galbreath, owner of the Pittsburgh Pirates, both owned racehorses. One of Galbreath's even won the Kentucky Derby.

Still, DeBartolo did not get the White Sox. Instead it went later to a pair of guys I didn't know at the time, Eddie Einhorn and Jerry Reinsdorf. When I asked about them, the message I got was "Be careful!" One guy told me that Einhorn was "a little czar who thinks he knows everything." And another friend told me that Reinsdorf thought I was anti-Semitic. It didn't look real promising.

So I said, "I think each ball club should have clinics for wives once a week on baseball because I don't think they know what the game of baseball really is." Then [Mike] Royko said something else in regard to them, and I added, "Oh, they were just horny broads that wanted to get married, and they wanted a little money, a little security, and they wanted a big, strong ball player."

11
EINHORN, REINSDORF, AND HORNY BROADS

Even czars turned ball club owners need radio and television announcers, and, after Reinsdorf learned that I had worked happily with Jewish people throughout my life and liked them no more or no less than anybody else in the world, I was rehired to work the booth with Harry Caray.

It was much the same under Einhorn and Reinsdorf as it had been under Veeck. They didn't want the product criticized either—it was always beautiful at the ball park, and the White Sox players were a faultless group. Three weeks after the 1981 season began, there was already talk that I was going to be fired. A Chicago sportswriter, Ron Rapoport of the *Sun-Times*, wrote, "Controversy follows him [me] the way May follows April." Several things prompted that remark. First, Einhorn spoke at a luncheon in Chicago and said he was upset about my criticism of the team, Tony LaRussa, and some of the White Sox players. He said it was a matter of "grave concern," which actually meant he was thinking of booting my ass out of the broadcast booth if I didn't adopt the warm, winning ways of a homer. Then a writer for *The Sporting News* wrote that I was trying to get LaRussa fired. I wasn't. In fact, as much as I disagreed with the way he managed, I never tried to get him fired. It was never my intention to get anyone fired.

It was around that time too that LaRussa went to Einhorn and Reinsdorf and told them that the problem with the White Sox, who then were in a losing streak, was the announcers, Harry and myself. We were second-guessing him, he said, and it was upsetting the ball players.

Reinsdorf called me down in Texas—we were on a road trip—and said he was flying down and would like to have lunch with me and maybe talk over a few things. This was all before the first week in May was over.

Well, Reinsdorf came down, and Harry and I sat down with him and Einhorn, and we had our little talk. They told me that they thought I was second-guessing their manager and that I had to stop it.

I told them that I didn't think they knew the definition of *second-guessing*. "If two pitchers were warming up," I said, "a right-hander and a left-hander, and LaRussa put in the left-hander and he got hit, and I said LaRussa should have put in the right-hander, that was second-guessing. Or if a batter bunted, and I said LaRussa should have called for a hit and run, that too was second-guessing." Harry and I didn't do that, however. We first-guessed. Then I explained what first-guessing was: Before a thing happened, I would say I'd like to see a bunt in this situation or I'd like to see an intentional walk here. That was first-guessing. It's nothing different from what the fan in the stands would do, I told them. Reinsdorf said, "Well, I don't want any second-guessing *or* first-guessing then."

I knew right then we were in trouble and that LaRussa had Reinsdorf wrapped around his little finger and also that LaRussa now had himself a pair of certified scapegoats. If LaRussa was as good a baseball man as he was a politician, the White Sox would have been a lot better for it. I understood that in early 1981.

The White Sox were not that bad a team in 1981, at least until the players' strike that year. Einhorn and Reinsdorf, unlike Veeck, had money to spend, and they went out and got Carlton Fisk and Greg Luzinski, two well-recognized, top-of-the-line ball players. When the players went on strike the Sox were 31 and 22, only 2½ games out of first place. It was in the second half of the season, when play resumed, that they really folded up. During that fiasco, they were 23 and 30 and ended up in sixth place in the American League West.

I got into it with the umpires again that year too. We were in the first game of a doubleheader with the California Angels at Comiskey Park. It was the third inning, and Mike Squires, the Sox first baseman, was at bat. He took a called third strike that had to be a foot outside. Everybody in the ball park knew it and let home plate umpire Joe Brinkman know it. I stood up to stretch in the broadcast booth, and Brinkman turned around and looked up for some reason or other. When I saw him looking up I held my two hands about a foot apart to show him that I thought the pitch was that far outside.

Brinkman then held his hands apart like I'd done and then gave a little Elvis-Presley-like swivel of his hips, I guess to show me what he thought of my opinion. I thought the whole thing was funny and that we had this little thing going, so I jerked my thumb up in a gesture as if to say, "You're out," or "You're out of the game."

Well, Dale Ford, the first base umpire, saw it and really got riled up. He started yelling something to Brinkman. Later they both said that I'd given Brinkman the finger. They were the only two people in the ball park or the press box or the broadcast booth who thought that. Harry Caray, who was sitting there next to me, went on record, saying, "I never saw Jimmy use any obscene gesture, and I was right there in the booth." And then he added this, which I liked a lot, "Besides, what are the umpires doing looking up in the booth? No wonder they blow so many plays."

Ford was so uptight that he told the Sox first base coach, Vada Pinson, that I was inciting the crowd against the umpires. That's why they were booing them. That was one of the most ridiculous things I ever heard come out of an umpire's mouth. Then he said that he was scheduled to be the home plate umpire in game two, and if I continued to be "so animated," he would forfeit the game to the Angels. That would have set an interesting precedent: from that day forward any thin-skinned umpire could just forfeit a game if a broadcaster or the fans disagreed on a call and let the ump know about it.

Brinkman was just as nuts about it the next day. He was quoted in the Chicago newspapers as saying I was "crazy." And he said, "We could have had a riot. There are 50,000 people out there. What happens if they decide to storm us from their seats?" And he called *me* crazy!

Then the umpires' association lawyers got into it again, the same goofy firm that threatened me before. They said they were discussing what kind of legal action they might want to take against me. I couldn't believe they would waste their time with this kind of nonsense. Maybe umpires and lawyers deserve each other.

After the strike was over, Einhorn and Reinsdorf decided that Harry and I should be split up. Lou Brock, the great base stealer in his time with the St. Louis Cardinals, was hired to work with Harry on television. I'd work with Harry for just two innings on the radio. All the rest of my broadcast time was to be with Joe McConnell. The reason they gave was that they felt Harry was getting me wound up, egging me on. One writer, Ray Sons of the *Chicago Sun-Times*, described it in a rather clever way, I thought.

"It's taking away the full moon [Caray] from Wolfman. When Harry's moon face shines on Jimmy, Piersall grows fangs and a fur coat and says anything that pops into his head. When Caray delivers a biting criticism, Piersall tops him." Sons also reminded Einhorn and Reinsdorf that they were in the entertainment business and that the new arrangement wasn't nearly as much fun for the fans as it had been with Harry and me teamed together.

If they thought that separating Harry and me was going to stop me from telling the truth about what was happening on the playing field, they were dead wrong. When I saw Greg Luzinski dogging it after hitting a ground ball in the infield, I said so. I complained that a guy making so many hundreds of thousands of dollars a year for playing baseball owed it to the fans to run out a ground ball. In that particular instance, the ball was bobbled, and he would have been safe if he had hustled.

LaRussa was so protective of his ball players that he defended Luzinski the next day. No matter what, it couldn't be a player's fault. It was Harry or me who was the problem, he would say. He'd find some cock-and-bull excuse for his player and then rant about how we were maligning his wonderful players. Well, he said that the reason Luzinski didn't really run it out was because his hamstring was bothering him and that he—LaRussa—had instructed Luzinski to take it easy so as not to aggravate the injury. What bullshit. A couple of innings later, when Luzinski doubled to drive in the winning run, he didn't dog it. He ran like hell. And what kind of managing would it be to put an injured player in a game and then tell him to take it easy, don't bother hustling? Pure unadulterated bullshit. But that's the way it was with LaRussa, a million excuses and a hurt little boy when somebody said one of his players loafed or goofed up. The fact of the matter is, if there was any truth to LaRussa's explanation, if Luzinski was in fact injured, then LaRussa should have told the media and the press that particular fact before the game started.

The biggest flak of that year, however, came after I appeared on Mike Royko's first television talk show. It was a new thing in Chicago; Royko, the city's great columnist, was going to host a TV show from a tavern called the Billy Goat, which was one of his favorite hangouts. The guy producing it called me up and said they'd like me to appear. Harry was going to be on the show, too.

I said, "Okay, I'll do it for five hundred bucks."

He said, "Hey, the other guys are all doing it for nothing."

"I don't care," I said. Actually, I didn't really want to go on it in the first place, which is why I asked for the money. I thought they'd just say no and forget about it. I don't like taverns or bars. I don't drink and never have. They're dark and smoky, and I don't like sitting around listening to all the bullshit that usually goes on in them.

The producer talked to Mike Royko and then called me back and said, "Okay, you've got the five hundred." Well, now I had to go. But I had some real misgivings, some premonitions that I might get myself in trouble. When I was leaving the house for it, I told Jan, "I really don't want to do this. I think it will just bring trouble." Was I ever right.

I didn't like it at all when I got to the Billy Goat tavern. It was hot in there and filled with smoke. It was crowded. Harry was there, and he was having a ball. And Royko was sitting there trying on toupees and kidding with people. But I didn't like the whole scene; it just was not my kind of place, my kind of lifestyle. I thought the world of Mike Royko, and he's probably the best newspaper writer in the country, but the whole idea of this television show made me nervous. I started to leave, in fact, but the producer caught up with me outside, and I went back.

Well, the show went on, and it was actually going very

well. Royko was saying a lot of things that I thought *he* was going to get in trouble with. So was Harry. I was worrying about *them*. At the same time I was having a good time kidding with Royko.

Then Mike asked, "How come the ball players' wives are always on your case?"

The question had to do with the fact that some of the wives would misinterpret some of the remarks made on the air by Harry and me. So I said, "I think each ball club should have clinics for wives once a week on baseball because I don't think they know what the game of baseball really is." Then Royko said something else in regard to them, and I added, "Oh, they were just horny broads that wanted to get married, and they wanted a little money, a little security, and they wanted a big, strong ball player."

Nothing big came out of it at the time. When I said it Royko didn't blink, just chuckled. I don't know if Harry even reacted to it. But there wasn't even a pause, and the show went on. It was nothing more than the kind of conversation that might be going on in a thousand different saloons in Chicago at the same time.

The next day, a Sunday, when I arrived at the ball park, I ran into Jerry Reinsdorf. The only thing he said to me was, "My wife and I really enjoyed you on that show last night." That was all; no comment about the "horny broads" statement. In fact, I didn't get anything on it for the next three or four days. But the trouble was brewing with LaRussa and the players. It was the kind of thing LaRussa needed to focus on me. He went to Einhorn and Reinsdorf and said something to the effect that he wouldn't bring the players on the field if I was up in the broadcast booth. That was his copout. He should have been worrying more about how his team was stinking up Comiskey Park. He couldn't handle that, though.

Later that week, I got to the ball park, and suddenly I was getting all kinds of calls. A guy from WMAQ radio said he had heard that I was getting fired, and all kinds of other calls like that came in. It was a night game, and a while before it a young kid came up to me and said, "They want to see you."

I said, "Who's they?"

He said, "Mr. Einhorn, in his office."

I walked in there, and several other people were there besides Einhorn. Reinsdorf was not at the ball park that night. Nobody said anything at first; there was just this kind of awkward silence. Then Einhorn said, "We'd like it if you didn't go on the show tonight."

"For what?" I said.

"Well, for what you said about the players' wives last Saturday. We'd like you off until we can get this thing straightened out."

That really ticked me off. I said, "Wait a minute. You told me before that I could say anything I wanted on other shows, off the White Sox network." Which he certainly had. "Aren't you a man of your word?" Then something inside told me not to say any more and just to get out of there.

When I stepped outside, the cameramen were already there ready to take pictures. Everybody knew I was off the air before I did.

Reinsdorf called me later, and I told him too that I thought it was real crummy, after having told me I could say what I wanted, to then suspend me for doing it. I yelled over the phone at him about the hypocrisy of it, but it didn't matter. He said that he and Einhorn wanted me to take a rest, a little vacation. I get more "rests" than anybody else on this planet, I think. There was nothing I could do but say okay, so Jan and I went up to a resort in Wisconsin to get away from it all.

Needless to say, everyone was talking about whether or not I'd be fired again. Some of the writers were on my side, others weren't. The man who went to bat hardest for me was the one with the biggest audience in the Chicago area, Mike Royko himself. He wrote:

"Piersall, with his friend Harry Caray as his straightman, was a remarkable guest. . . . He talked about baseball. . . . He talked openly about his past mental problems. . . . He talked about his philosophy of life.

"And he made a couple of bawdily funny remarks about players' wives."

Royko said that I was "a no-BS person" and then pointed out what I had said on his show: "If you are honest and open in your opinions, somebody up there will try to nail you." (I was fast finding out what good carpenters Einhorn and Reinsdorf were.)

Royko also said, "And in Piersall's occupation—sports broadcasting—we have some of the world's mealiest mealymouths. If a football player ever whipped out a switchblade knife and cut the throat of an opposing player, the announcer would probably say, "Well, there's a little temper flare-up down there."

Then he took off on the little carpenters, Einhorn and Reinsdorf. "After the TV show was aired, many friends, acquaintances, and strangers gave me their opinions.

"The majority said the highlight of the show was the Piersall interview. They were impressed by him for most of the reasons I mentioned above.

"None found his remarks about players' wives offensive. They recognized that he was just popping off for a laugh.

"So if you [Einhorn and Reinsdorf] fire him, you'll be admitting that (a) you can't tolerate an honest man; (b) you have no sense of humor; (c) you have no sense of proportion, and (d) you are pillars in the age of mealymouths."

That was the mild column.

At the end of it, he invited Einhorn and Reinsdorf to appear on his next show with me and an assembly of 100 diehard White Sox fans. When they declined he really went after them, referring to them as "Einsdorf and

Reinhorn" in one place, "Reinsdorn and Einsdort" in another, and "Reinshoof or Eindoon" in still another.

He wrote, "They don't think that Piersall, in speaking his mind, has conveyed the 'image' they think is 'appropriate.'

"That concern about 'image' is an ominous sign for the future. What will they do next—forbid players from readjusting or scratching their athletic supporters while on the field, tell them they can't spit, or otherwise tamper with these and other sacred traditions of the great game?"

In regard to the whole thing about the players' wives, he said, "The point that Piersall and Harry Caray had made on the show was that the players don't know what is being said about them in the broadcast booth because they are down on the field.

"But when they get home—tired and foot-weary after a hard three hours of earning their $200,000 a year, wanting only to have a beer and a pleasant night's sleep of dreaming about making $400,000 a year—what do they get?

"They get a wife yammering: 'Do you know what Piersall said about you tonight? He said that you really fouled up when that fly ball missed your glove and bounced off your forehead. Are you going to take that kind of unfair criticism?'

"No wonder the Sox have been losing. They're probably filled with terrible stress at having to go home and be nagged about what Piersall said about them.

"Rather than creating a silly furor, the players' wives should devote their energies to such proper baseball-wifely pursuits as brushing their mink coats and checking out the current interest rates on T-bills."

It was all very funny—and very true. And Einhorn and Reinsdorf hated it. The more Royko wrote on my behalf, the deeper I sank into trouble with the two of them. Royko didn't know it, of course, and he couldn't have done anything to change their petty ways anyway.

Meanwhile, with my fate being pondered by the two who told me I could say anything I wanted on the air, I decided to release a statement. After the thing had blown up, I regretted having used the term "horny broads" on the air. But I hadn't said "White Sox players' wives"; I had just made a generalization and didn't mean anyone in particular. I really didn't feel I was wrong, but still I felt I ought to go on record with an apology, hoping to ease the thing.

It was a very short press conference, but a large one. It was so big, in fact—about 200 media people and writers showed up—that they had to hold it down on the playing field at Comiskey Park. I simply said:

"I never intended to offend anyone with my remarks on the 'Mike Royko Show.' Being at a bar for one of the few times in my life, I was trying to have fun. It was never my intention to hurt anyone. If my remarks offended anyone, I am sorry. I only meant them to be funny and didn't really think before I spoke. If I offended players and their wives all over the country, I am sorry. I have seven grown daughters of my own and wouldn't like to think I offended them. Please don't ask me any questions. This is the only statement I will make."

Harry Caray, as usual, stood up for me. He told the press, "You're damned right I'm standing up there with Jimmy. If they fire him, they might as well fire us both. I don't give a crap. If they're not going to fire him, they ought to let him alone. If they are, if they don't want him around, then let him go right now. But don't leave Jimmy hanging on a mountaintop. It seems they've always got him on a precipice, hanging by his fingertips. . . . Don't they know the fans want Jimmy and me together again?"

As a matter of fact, I got a lot of support from a lot of different corners—Bill Gleason on the sports pages; Gary Deeb, the radio/TV columnist; and old friend Don Drysdale, former great pitcher for the Dodgers, Hall of Famer now, who was then doing the color for the California Angels and ABC's "Monday Night Baseball." Don was quoted by Deeb as saying:

"But I have lots of respect for announcers with different styles. For instance, I pick up [baseball] on the cable from Chicago, and I love to watch the White Sox games with Harry Caray and Jimmy Piersall. I sit there and just laugh my head off when those two guys get going. They can be very critical of the team, but they're almost always right.

"I'd hate like hell to see Jim get fired. Jimmy is basically a nice guy. I've known him a long, long time, and believe me, he just doesn't know how to lie—not even to protect himself. He's totally honest. Other people may say things more diplomatically, but Jimmy just comes right out and lets it rip."

There were only a couple of weeks left in the season at that point. The decision from Einhorn and Reinsdorf was that I would be suspended for the duration, with pay. I'd never heard of anyone being suspended *with* pay before, but I wasn't going to question it. I suppose they hoped it would make them look better to the fans, like some sort of wonderful, charitable guys. The truth of the matter was that they suspended me for doing something that they had gone on record as saying that I could in fact do.

That was it for 1981. Not the best of years for me.

Then the wait began again. There was no rush to my door with a contract for the 1982 season. And for the first time there wasn't for Harry either.

Harry didn't wait around, however. In November 1982, a press conference was called in the Ambassador East Hotel in Chicago, and the Cubs announced that their new broadcaster, to replace Jack Brickhouse who had just retired, was none other than Harry Caray.

Earlier that morning, Harry had called me to tell me what was going to happen. "I honestly believe this will help you," he said. "I certainly hope it will."

The White Sox had made Harry an offer, but they also had waited too long. He was fed up with all their crap, and he turned them down. I wished him the best on his move to the other side of town.

I would miss Harry, no doubt about that. As I said to the press, "A lot of good things come to an end. He's the best. And I'm indebted to him for learning what I've learned. We had good chemistry together. These have been very memorable years for me."

Memorable and stormy, I guess you might say.

*If I had done what [Tony] LaRussa did,
they would have been clamoring to have
me put in a sanitarium. . . . I felt LaRussa
was not rational, and I felt sorry for him.
But I didn't think it should simply be
hushed up. What I did then was to tell
about the incident the next night on my
SportsVision show. I described what had
happened and then said, "He [LaRussa]
showed me no class by not facing me alone.
He came with two other people. I feel sorry
for the Sox. I feel sorry for a guy, who, in
baseball terms, is totally bush."*

12
MIDNIGHT CALLERS, "SCUM," AND SURVIVING

After Harry Caray made his move to the north side of Chicago, the White Sox hired a new broadcast team. For very big money, they got Don Drysdale, who had been on the air for the Angels, and Ken "Hawk" Harrelson, who had been broadcasting the Boston Red Sox games. It would seem that that would have ended my broadcasting career with the White Sox.

But it didn't. Now in the White Sox plan was SportsVision, a cable TV subscription package engineered by Eddie Einhorn. The White Sox would be on pay TV most of the year—112 games would be broadcast exclusively on SportsVision, and subscribers would have to come up with $21.95 a month, year-round, for it.

Needless to say, a lot of the fans weren't too wild about it, suddenly having to pay that kind of dough for the privilege of watching their team play when in the past they had watched them for nothing.

But for me, it was not going to be a bad thing. I met with

Einhorn, and he told me that there was going to be a place for me in the new scheme of things even though they'd hired Drysdale and Harrelson for a couple of hundred thousand dollars a year apiece (and each got a *five-year* contract).

The reason there was a place for me was because Einhorn had to do anything and everything in his power to sell the idea of SportsVision to White Sox fans. He knew I had a name and a good following among the fans. He felt it would make SportsVision more palatable to the fans, that I would draw viewers.

I knew that. He knew that. Everybody involved knew it. As a result, I told him I wanted more money than I'd been making.

Einhorn leaned across the table and said to me, "You're not a professional."

"How the hell do you figure that?" I said. Then I reached into my pocket and pulled out a handful of bills, maybe five hundred dollars. "You pay me. And when I've got that in my pocket for going on the air, I'm a professional." Then I added, "Who do you think the fans would listen to, who would they *want* to listen to, from the broadcast booth, you or me?"

"You couldn't get a job in another city," he said.

"Who knows? Maybe you're right. But I am a pro, and I've got a following in *this* city."

We went back and forth for a while like that. Our meetings were never the model of low-key, relaxed get-togethers. I have to admit Einhorn was always a ballsy guy. He had some very good traits, too. He knew how to raise money, knew how to make people believe in a thing, and he got jobs done. I have to give him credit for those things.

At that meeting, we finally got down to the reason I was there. Einhorn said they had a contract offer for me for 1982.

By this time, I'd hired an agent for the first time in my

life. I got Jack Childers, one of the most prominent in the country and a guy who had represented a huge stable of athletes in all sports. Over the years, he'd handled things for names like Kareem Abdul Jabbar, Pete Rose, Lou Brock, Dick Butkus, Keith Hernandez. He would handle the contract negotiations with Einhorn and Reinsdorf for me.

The outcome was a contract with good money, but again it was only for one year. Childers worked out all the details, and one, I felt, was very important. There was a unique clause. Jack Childers explained it at the press conference, announcing the entire new White Sox broadcasting setup. "He can say anything he wants to, and he can't be fired," Childers told the media and the press. "There will be no more suspensions."

Eddie Einhorn, at the same press conference, agreed that it was true. No gags or muzzles now. Piersal is free to "do his thing," Einhorn said. "He has a guaranteed contract where this independence is spelled out."

Jerry Reinsdorf came up to me after the press conference and told me he wanted to talk to me. He took me over into another room where we could be alone and said, "I know you're probably not happy with just a one-year contract, but if you do well, we'll take care of you."

The kind of work I was to do for SportsVision was in the manner of what Brent Musberger does for NFL football on Sundays. I would be back in the studios, not at the ballpark. I would have a commentary show before the game and after it, and I would do 90-second spots throughout the game, between innings. It was a tough schedule, the most demanding form of broadcasting I'd yet encountered.

Besides SportsVision, I was also hired to do a radio show after each game for WMAQ. When I finished up the SportsVision postgame show I'd go downstairs in their studios where a special microphone was set up so I could go right into the radio show. It was a call-in show and could run anywhere from 15 to 45 minutes. I was going to be a very busy person. But the money was good, there were to be no restrictions, and I was, in truth, delighted with the whole arrangement.

I told the press and the media, "Gentlemen, I'm just glad to be employed. And you won't find any change in me. They [the White Sox] better play well. At the salaries they're making, if these players don't go out on the field and perform the way I feel the fans, who are forking up $21.95 a month, deserve to have them perform, I'll let you know about it. We've got some players who are exciting, and some who are not exciting. I'll report the good and the bad, just like old times." I wanted to be sure no one thought I might be mellowing out any.

In the beginning at SportsVision, it was a real mess, which is understandable, I guess, because the thing was brand-new. It was hectic, in fact. I'd call for a tape and nobody could find it, or they'd put on the wrong one. We got through the growing pains together, however. Einhorn was never around. There weren't any meetings. No one bothered me. I had no problems as a result. I just went on the air and, as Einhorn had said, "did my thing."

As always, I told it like it happened on the field. I reported. Everybody who followed the White Sox knew I was around. Ray Sons wrote in the *Chicago Sun-Times*, "Piersall is as obscure as Howard Cosell's nose."

The team was an improved one in 1982, but there were still a lot of flaws. Foremost among them was Ron LeFlore. "He's stinking up the ballpark," I said, and that was about the kindest thing that could have been said about the way he was fielding and bunting that year. I mean he got hit in the head trying to catch a routine fly ball. But then I said about Harold Baines, "What a thrill for me last year to see him come around as a fielder. He's the best right fielder in the game right now." The bad and the good, equal time!

I heard no complaints from either Einhorn or Reinsdorf. Sure, the players moped around and complained if I pointed out that one of them ought to spend some time practicing his bunting so he could come up to doing it like a major leaguer or that another player was just not hustling out there.

But the one person I obviously upset the most was the manager, Tony LaRussa. He was the world's leading cry-baby, an excuse-maker without parallel. He had tried before to blame his problems and the mistakes of his ball players on Harry Caray and myself. We had said at the time, "Hey, Tony, we're not the ones misjudging the fly balls; we're not the ones getting picked off first base; we're not the ones trotting around when we're supposed to be hustling." But he always felt that any ill on the field was a direct result of Harry's or my criticizing mistakes or mental errors or simply bad plays. Now Harry was gone and I was the only one left. He would have to focus all his attention on me.

The simple fact of the matter was that Tony LaRussa just could not stand the heat in the proverbial kitchen. That became abundantly clear to me the night that he came down to the SportsVision studios with two of his coaches to confront me in late July that year.

The team was doing lousy around that time, and there was a lot of talk about LaRussa being dumped. The White Sox were about eight games out, and the pressures were coming down on LaRussa from all sides. Since the All-Star break, they were a miserable 4 and 12. The fans booed him constantly, he was getting bad press, and there was no visible or vocal support from Einhorn and Reinsdorf. And the two of them had not been critical of my criticisms of LaRussa's managing ability (or lack of ability, I should say). Their silence at both ends could be taken as an indictment of him and a hint that his job was far from secure.

THE TRUTH HURTS

To put it in the proper light, here is a sample opening paragraph from an article in the *Chicago Sun-Times,* written by Dave van Dyck around that time. "Tony LaRussa may not have kept the boo-birds off his back Friday, but he kept his job for another day. . . ." That was the climate in Chicago then.

Even LaRussa was quoted in the same edition of the *Sun-Times* as saying, "I wouldn't give me a vote of confidence either. . . . I'm paid to win; we haven't won." And he added, "I know if I saw it [the White Sox record], I would be concerned."

So he decided to take his frustrations out on me.

I'll remember that night as long as I live. It was July 29th, a Thursday, and the White Sox had just lost another ball game, this one to the Boston Red Sox. I'd finished my SportsVision show after the game and had then gone downstairs to the other studio to handle the call-in show on WMAQ radio. When it was over, the WMAQ producer, Richard Waldo, came in and said that LaRussa was outside with a couple of his coaches, looking for me. He said that they had forced their way in. Security wasn't able to stop them because they said they had an appointment with me and had just gone on in. Waldo also said that LaRussa had asked if there was a back entrance to the studios.

I knew they hadn't come down at midnight for a little social chitchat. But I went out into the hall anyway, and there were LaRussa and Jim Leyland, the Sox third base coach. Charlie Lau, their batting coach, was also in the studio, but he wasn't in the hall. He was upstairs watching the door to see that nobody came in. That didn't really matter because Richard Waldo was still there as a witness, and he was not going to leave.

LaRussa came up to me, and he had the worst look on his face. His eyes were wild. He said to me, "You're a liar."

"What did I lie about?"

He didn't know what to say at first. I mean he was not

rational. He said, "You lied about [Chet] Lemon." Then he said, "You tried to get Leyland fired."

"That's bullshit," I said.

"You said he couldn't coach the outfield."

"I didn't even know he was coaching the outfield. But if he is, then I'd say it's right, he can't. That's my opinion."

Well, with that, Leyland took a couple of steps toward me, screaming at me and pulling at his shirt. He tore the damn thing off, his own shirt. He was a wild man; something just snapped, and he went bananas. But it didn't last. I didn't go for him, which I think is what both LaRussa and Leyland wanted. I just stood there, and that's as far as it went. They weren't going to do something with Richard Waldo standing there as a witness.

Then LaRussa started shouting again. This time he said that I got Ron Schueler, their former pitching coach, fired.

"That's crazy," I said. "I didn't try to get anybody fired. And in the first place I couldn't get somebody fired."

"I'm gonna get you down the road," LaRussa said. "Down the road I'm gonna make things tough for you."

"You better get out of here," I finally said. And they did leave then. There wasn't anything else they could do with a witness there. They had not been able to provoke me into a fight, which I'm sure was their purpose in coming down there. That way they could get me fired, and the pair of them or the three, if Lau came down too, could have beat the crap out of me. I suppose that would have made them happy. The whole idea of the three of them coming down to the studios to confront me at midnight was something right out of high school. The whole thing was loony. And did they stop to think that I had had open-heart surgery, a triple bypass? That maybe I could have had a heart attack as a result of their little foray? It was not just sad; it was sick. If I had done what LaRussa did, they would have been clamoring to have me put in a sanitarium.

There were a lot of things I could have done afterward.

THE TRUTH HURTS

I could have called the police. I was a member of the media being harassed and threatened by three men. I could have taken it directly to the baseball commissioner. And that would have gotten LaRussa and his two buddies in a whole helluva lot of trouble. But I didn't do either. I felt LaRussa was not rational, and I felt sorry for him. But I didn't think it should simply be hushed up.

What I did then was to tell about the incident the next night on my SportsVision show. I described what had happened and then said, "He [LaRussa] showed me no class by not facing me alone. He came with two other people. I feel sorry for the Sox. I feel sorry for a guy, who, in baseball terms, is totally bush."

After that broadcast, both Einhorn and Reinsdorf called me and apologized for LaRussa. LaRussa should have, but he didn't because, as I said, he had no class. But both the owners did, and they congratulated me on the way I handled myself in the situation. Einhorn said, "You're a pro now, Jimmy." And in the newspapers Einhorn was quoted as saying about me and my assessments of LaRussa, "It's his job. He's giving his opinion. That's the way it [SportsVision] is set up. He's been saying some good things about him [LaRussa], too. He's done his job."

When the 1982 season was over, Einhorn told me that I'd done a good job. He said everybody was pleased and that *this year*, meaning 1983, I would have my contract by October 5th. I thought, wonderful. No more waiting through the winter, wondering if I would even have a job after the snow melted in Chicago; no more wondering if I should pack a bag for Sarasota and spring training or if I should get out and start looking for a job somewhere else.

Jack Childers, my agent, sat down with Einhorn and Reinsdorf, and they hashed it out. It was to be the best contract I ever had: good money and two years, guaranteed. Again, I could say what I wanted on the air, and they couldn't fire me. I could be taken off the air, sure, but I'd still get paid for the two years of the contract.

But October 5th came and went, and there was no contract for me to sign.

Details had to be worked out, everyone said. A little thing here, a little thing there. But always, it was coming. Just relax, be patient.

Winter came, and still there was no contract. Dave Martin, the general manager at WMAQ radio, said he would like me to do a sports show for him on Monday nights. I really didn't want to do it. Premonitions maybe. But because I didn't have a signed contract and I wasn't doing anything else, I said why not, I'd do it.

One Monday night in March, a caller asked me about the trade that Rollie Hemond and Dallas Green, the general managers of the White Sox and the Cubs, had just made. It involved Steve Trout and a bunch of other players, and it was one that seemed overwhelmingly beneficial to the Sox. The caller asked, "Did the White Sox hold a gun to Dallas Green's head to get him to make that trade?"

"There's no one in the White Sox organization smart enough to hold a gun to anyone's head," I said. And as soon as I said it, I knew I shouldn't have. I didn't mean it the way it came out. What I meant was that nobody would think of doing something like that. It was just a quick, pop answer to a question that was phrased in a goofy way.

Nothing came of it, at least for a while. About two weeks later, though, the White Sox front office got a letter and a tape recording from a priest. In the letter, the priest said that he was fed up with my comments about the White Sox front office. He sent the tape along as an example, and it included the remark I'd made about no one being smart in the White Sox organization.

It was shunted on to Einhorn, and you can imagine what hit the fan. Einhorn and Reinsdorf called me in for a meeting, and Jack Childers went along with me.

They said, "We want you to listen to this," and then they

played the tape recording. One of them asked after it was over if I had really said that.

"Yeah, I did," I said. "I'm not happy about it, but I said it."

They said that if that was the way I truly felt about the organization, I should not be accepting the contract that they had offered (which, however, still had not materialized). "If you don't like the way we operate, you shouldn't be working for us," they said.

"Well, I said it. Didn't mean it the way it came out. What else can I tell you?"

Jack Childers argued my case with them then, and the bottom line was that it would be dropped, forgotten, and that they would proceed with getting the contract finalized. This was the same contract, incidentally, that Einhorn had said I would have by October 5, 1982, the one still to be finalized now in March 1983.

In Sarasota, there were some flaps about spring training. According to my boss Jack Jacobson, at SportsVision, I was supposed to do some work for them down in Florida. But after the run-in regarding the tape, Einhorn told me he didn't need me for anything during spring training.

But I had also struck a separate deal myself with WMAQ radio to do stuff for them from spring training, and they were paying me expense money.

But then, while I was down in Sarasota, Mike Klein, the producer at SportsVision called and asked me to do 35 shows from down there. They were what they called "baseball event shows," which were interviews and pieces we taped that would be used on the air at different times during March.

So I got right to it and, bang, I knocked them out in two weeks. According to my previous contract, I was to get $800 a show—that's $28,000 for the package. For a guy who, according to Einhorn, wasn't needed to do anything at spring training, a $28,000 deal wasn't too bad. I enjoyed sending them the bill.

At the same time, Tony LaRussa was trying his damnedest to prevent me from getting press credentials. Without them I could not get on the field or into the clubhouse. He couldn't deny me those, of course, but it didn't stop him from trying.

At any rate, I went ahead and did the things I was supposed to at spring training for SportsVision. About the contract, the story was still the same throughout. It was coming. Einhorn had been so busy, traveling so much, that he hadn't had a chance to sign it. But he would.

On opening day, which in 1983 was down in Texas against the Rangers, I still hadn't gotten it. I said I wouldn't go on the air without it, that the whole thing had reached an absolutely ridiculous stage. But they talked me into going on anyway. I was not happy about the situation, but I did it. The whole thing about the contract had been bothering me tremendously—I was up there on that mountaintop, like Harry Caray had said; they had me hanging from that precipice by my fingertips again.

Anyway, I did both the SportsVision and WMAQ shows from the studios in Chicago. The Sox looked bad that night and lost 5–3. I had made some comments criticizing LaRussa for starting rookie Greg Walker instead of Mike Squires at first base, and for starting Tom Paciorek in left instead of Ron Kittle. There were some other critical comments during my postgame show. And I also said something like the White Sox, despite what the organization thinks, are a team whose future is next year, not this year.

I suspected I was in trouble when I heard the next day that Reinsdorf had asked for the tapes of both my SportsVision shows and the WMAQ call-in program. I found out just how much trouble a few hours before I was to do my pregame show that day. Reinsdorf came down to the SportsVision offices himself, called me in, and told me I was fired.

I was crying mad. I had been jacked around long enough. It had taken a toll on me.

179

THE TRUTH HURTS

The next day, after thinking about it most of a sleepless night, I realized that the whole thing was just a copout. They had been looking for a reason to get rid of me. Why else would they have stalled off my "guaranteed" contract so long?

What I had said on the air that night of the opening game wasn't any different really from the kinds of things I'd said the year before. And my contract the year before and the one that never did show up in 1983 guaranteed me the right to say what I wanted on the air—to express my opinions. And that's the very thing they fired me for, expressing my opinions about what was going on down on the field.

It was a cruel way to handle it, I thought. Why did they have to wait until opening day? Why didn't they just do it back in October so I would have time to try to find another job?

I felt I had kept the faith with myself and the fans. Einhorn and Reinsdorf knew that I was a guy who called it like he saw it. They knew I had a poor opinion of the quality of the management of the ball club. There was nothing new there.

The irony of the whole thing was that the morning after I got fired, my agent, Jack Childers, got a call from Einhorn's lawyers saying that the contract was finally ready and he could pick it up later that afternoon. Childers told them that it didn't matter anymore. They asked what he meant. He just shook his head and told them to go talk to their clients.

I still had the WMAQ job, however, so the White Sox would not be rid of me altogether. Dave Martin, my boss at WMAQ, was a strong, loyal supporter and said that under no circumstances would I be let go, even if pressures were exerted by the White Sox front office. In fact, the day after I was fired from SportsVision, WMAQ took out additional ads promoting my show and emphasizing that now I would be heard "exclusively" on WMAQ.

MIDNIGHT CALLERS, "SCUM," AND SURVIVING

So I spent the 1983 season fielding calls on the radio about the White Sox, commenting on the good and the bad, no doubt antagonizing the thin-skinned Tony La-Russa. I couldn't be too critical, however, because the White Sox virtually romped through the American League West, an accomplishment even if it was in what was by far the worst division in major league baseball.

When the Sox won it, I said publicly that I congratulated the team and the organization and that I wished them well in the playoffs and hopefully the World Series too.

Harry Caray did the same thing. He said, "Everyone's happy for the White Sox, and no one's happier than I am. Here I am on the other side of the fence, and I'm ecstatic. Sure I wish it were the Cubs who were winning, but I've been talking on our games about how great a day it'll be for the city of Chicago and the Chicago fans when the Sox clinch it. I'm tickled to death for them."

What was the classy reaction from the White Sox management when they won it? When Jerry Reinsdorf was asked what he thought Harry and I might be thinking about their success, he said, "Wherever they are, they're eating their hearts out. I hope people realize what scum they are." A real nice sentiment, Jerry. A class answer. Just the kind of thing that all big businessmen, diplomats, team owners, sophisticates would say in their moment of glory. It was about equal in class to the comment Eddie Einhorn made during the season when the ball club was in a losing streak: "Maybe Tony LaRussa should pick another fight with Piersall," he said to Jerome Holtzman of the *Chicago Tribune*. "After that we won 17 out of 18."

It was a real pity that they could not enjoy their success without acting like vindictive little kids. Their statements define pretty clearly the kind of class they had.

Dave Martin left WMAQ radio before the 1982 season ended and was replaced as general manager by Tom Hoyt. I was assured my show would go on, that my job was as

181

secure as could be. Hoyt even told the press in late October that a one-year contract was being drawn up and would be signed by both parties before Thanksgiving. Where had I heard that kind of thing before?

Hoyt told it all to Jim O'Donnell, a Chicago area sports writer, and it appeared in *The Daily Herald.* "Jimmy is a talented guy," Hoyt said, "who knows a lot about baseball, and we want him back." When asked if he thought there might be objections to rehiring me by Eddie Einhorn and Jerry Reinsdorf, Hoyt said, "We have a very good relationship with the White Sox, and there will be no change in that. We don't tell them how to run their baseball team, and they don't tell us how to run our radio station. Jimmy is an employee of WMAQ."

Then he added, "We're looking at ideas about expanding the pregame or postgame shows, or adding to the morning-drive or afternoon-drive coverage of the Sox next season, and we plan to have Jimmy involved in all or part of that."

A little over *one week* later, Hoyt called me into the WMAQ offices and told me that my contract would not be renewed.

Fired again. Hoyt tried to come up with reasons to explain why he had so abruptly had a change of heart, mind, and plans. He said that, of course, pressures from the White Sox had nothing to do with it. Eddie Einhorn said that *they* certainly had nothing to do with it. Heavens, who would have ever thought that?

I was hurt, needless to say. I regretted losing the association with WMAQ because there were a lot of fine people there. At least the station gave me enough time to look for another job.

I found that WIND radio in Chicago was not afraid to hire me. I signed for a nightly talk and call-in show covering all sports.

After the WMAQ firing, I said to the press, "I am a survivor." And I knew that I would survive that particular blow.

What the firing did, in fact, do was bring to a close Part 2 of the Jimmy Piersall Story. There will be a Part 3; I guarantee it.